An Enabling Humility

An Enabling Humility:
Marianne Moore,
Elizabeth Bishop,
and the Uses of
Tradition

Jeredith Merrin

RUTGERS UNIVERSITY PRESS
New Brunswick and London

Library of Congress Cataloging-in-Publication Data

Merrin, Jeredith, 1944–
    An enabling humility : Marianne Moore, Elizabeth Bishop, and the
uses of tradition / Jeredith Merrin.
      p.   cm.
    Includes bibliographical references.
    ISBN 0-8135-1547-5
    1. American poetry—Women authors—History and criticism.
2. Feminism and literature—United States—History—20th century.
3. Women and literature—United States—History—20th century.
4. American poetry—20th century—History and criticism. 5. Moore,
Marianne, 1887–1972—Criticism and interpretation. 6. Bishop,
Elizabeth, 1911–1979—Criticism and interpretation. 7. Influence
(Literary, artistic, etc.) I. Title.
PS310.F45M47 1990
811′.5099287—dc20   89-70037
                                                          CIP

British Cataloging-in-Publication information available

For Diane Furtney,
and in memory of my father, Zachary Merrin

Contents

Acknowledgments

/

I WOULD LIKE TO THANK Professor Robert Pinsky, Professor Carol T. Christ, and Professor Susan Schweik for reading and commenting on earlier drafts of this book. Special thanks go to Lisa Sommer Merrin for her enthusiastic support.

Special thanks also to The Rosenbach Museum and Library in Philadelphia, Pennsylvania, for assistance and for permission to quote from selected passages of unpublished Marianne Moore correspondence and drafts; Marianne C. Moore, Marianne Moore's literary executor, for use of unpublished Moore materials; Patricia C. Willis, former curator of the Rosenbach Museum and Library, for her generous assistance with and support of early stages of this project; the Vassar College Library Rare Books and Manuscripts Division for assistance and for permission to quote from selected passages of unpublished Elizabeth Bishop correspondence and notebooks; Alice Methfessel, Elizabeth Bishop's literary executor, for use of unpublished Bishop materials.

An earlier version of Chapter 1 appeared in *Poesis,* Vol. 6, No. 1; an earlier version of Chapter 3 appeared in *Marianne Moore: Woman and Poet* (Orono: National Poetry Foundation, 1990).

An Enabling Humility

Introduction:
An Enabling Humility

HOW DOES A GIFTED WOMAN enable her own literary work in the midst of a male-predominant culture and in response to what was and still is a male-preponderant canon? This book addresses that question by considering how two of the most gifted twentieth-century American women poets made use of the Anglo-American literary tradition, and particularly of their Renaissance and Romantic precursors. Marianne Moore and Elizabeth Bishop do not stand here for *all* women writers. Indeed, it is part of my point that sweeping statements about what necessarily characterizes all male or all female authorship, about so-called and neatly separated patriarchal or matriarchal traditions, are ill-advised when we are speaking about the alembic of the imagination. Questions, though, as to how gendered experience may affect the activities of reading and writing I do consider as both crucial and fruitful. In these pages I pay attention to the ways in which both Moore and Bishop, whose aesthetic achievements now appear incontestable, managed to enable their projects by valuing as well as *revaluing* earlier contributions to what T. S. Eliot called "the common inheritance."[1] Finally, I argue in my concluding chapter, these "individual talents' " adaptations of and re-visions of male-authored works are significantly related to their gender and exhibit feminist commitment rather than self-serving collusion with patriarchal culture, female self-assurance rather than male-placating poetic insurance.

When I became happily and seriously engaged with Moore and Bishop at the beginning of my graduate career in 1980–81, their reputations in the academy did not then seem so clearly (as Harold Bloom has recently pronounced them) "beyond dispute."[2] Although admired and accepted by new-critically trained—and for the most part male—critics more than other women writers of their respective generations, Moore and Bishop still were generally regarded as peripheral to the first- and second-generation modernist canon. Professors appeared to perceive Moore, when they acknowledged her, as humorously eccentric: a fussy, spinsterish priestess of polite description and syllabic prosody. Students imbibed the notion that Bishop (even more rarely studied) was inoffensive and tidy, writing coolly on slight subjects with "a good eye for detail."[3] On the other hand, newly emergent feminist critics, understandably preferring to champion the brilliantly fierce, acid confessionalism of Plath and Sexton, the woman-celebrating poetry and bold early polemic of Adrienne Rich, either omitted Moore and Bishop from their discussions or mentioned them contemptuously in passing as women who wrote "to please men"— fainthearted females, each of whom in her own way tried, as one early feminist critic wrote of Moore, to be "one of the boys."[4]

My feeling that they were not being well served is part of the motivation behind these pages. While these two writers seemed to me remarkably fresh, they did not seem unrooted in or oblique to major concerns in Anglo-American literature.[5] Neither did they by any means fit the disparaging feminist description that would link them together as male-propitiating copycats or "good girls."

There are other, better reasons to link the two poets. They remained, after all, close friends from 1934 (Bishop then twenty-three, Moore forty-seven), until Marianne Moore's death on February 5, 1972. Despite their age difference, with Bishop having little yet to show in the way of finished work, and despite their having ostensibly little in common besides a Seven Sisters background, they quickly developed a close friendship, which from the outset was literary. They were brought together by Moore's friend, the Vassar College librarian Fanny Borden, after Bishop had inquired of Miss Borden why there was no copy of Moore's *Observations* on the shelf; their first meeting was outside the reading room of the New York Public Library. Cementing their friendship in her first letter to Moore, dated March 19, 1934, Bishop singled out two books she felt appropriate, recommending a new, "wonderful book" on tattooing and taking the liberty of sending Moore "the life of Hopkins by Father Lahey"—a revealing choice.[6] Because over the years Bishop was a globe-trotter, Moore a stay-at-home, the two kept in touch largely through letters. To read their correspondence (housed at Vassar College in Poughkeepsie, New York, and at the Rosenbach Museum and Library in Philadelphia) is to observe the evolution of an enviable literary relationship—one marked more by "nurture," as Bonnie Costello has pointed out, than by any Bloomian, agonistic notion of influence.[7] From its inception, the affectionate epistolary exchange is marked by mutual praise, entertaining passages of virtuoso description, cheerfully conspiratorial literary-critical jibes, judgments and anecdotes, by liberal humor and, when appropriate, liberal commiseration. To give some of the flavor, and to introduce some recurrent themes of the Moore/Bishop relationship, here is part of a letter, dated February 19, 1940, from Elizabeth to Marianne (one of Moore's poems had just been rejected by *The New Yorker*):

> What I think about the NEW YORKER can only be expressed like this: # ! @ ! ! ! @ # ! !

> And thank you for the marvellous postcard, and the very helpful comments on The Fish. I did as you suggested about everything except "breathing in" (if you can remember that) which I decided to leave as it was. "Lousy" is now "infested," and "gunwales"—which I had meant to be pronounced "gunn'l's" is "gunnels"—which is also correct according to the dictionary, and makes it plainer. I left off the outline of capitals, too, and feel very ADVANCED. I'm enclosing another poem that I'm afraid isn't very good—I just can't tell any more—

> Thank you so much for the "Glass Eye and Supplies"—I think I remember hearing Louise tell you once how fond I am of glass eyes—it is a story I'm afraid you will think a little indelicate. I used to have relatives with glass eyes when I was small and for some reason I worried because I thought they wouldn't go to Heaven. I don't think I was ever fully reassured until I read in Herbert something about—

> > "Taught me to live here so, that still one eye
> > Should aim and shoot at that which is on high . . ."[8]

This charming letter (which alludes to the glass eye of the author's maternal, Canadian grandmother and recalls to me the stuffed loon's glass eye in Bishop's later poem "First Death in Nova Scotia") points up Moore and Bishop's early, mentor/protégée relationship.[9] It shows the young Bishop's considered acquiescence to Moore's valued artistic advice, on the one hand; on the other hand, since she decides not to change the phrase "breathing in," her capacity for gentle self-assertion. This need to hold her own ground—not unlike, if perhaps milder than, a maturing daughter's necessary rebellion against her mother—would escalate six months later in the now-famous correspondence surrounding Bishop's poem "Roosters." There Bishop diplomatically declines the alternative title that Moore, always aloof to vulgar connotations, had offered, saying: "And for the same reason [a desire to emphasize "the essential baseness of militarism"] I want to keep as the title the rather contemptuous word ROOSTERS rather than the more classical COCK[S]." She also rejects politely but firmly Moore's other suggestions for her poem, including radical cuts, drastic revision of the poem's tercet structure, and omission of the term (to Marianne Moore offensively indecorous) "water-closet."[10]

The "glass eyes" letter quoted earlier suggests too the young poet's determination to learn by example and make her own poetry what Moore's indubitably was: modern, "ADVANCED." Though lighthearted, it reveals Bishop's need for reassurance about her own talent (which Moore supplied throughout their correspondence unstintingly).[11] It evinces slightly amused allowance for the older poet's extreme propriety ("a story I'm afraid you will think indelicate"), and a characteristic association on Bishop's part of early childhood with issues of Christian faith and anxiety, along with admiration for the seventeenth-century devotional poetry of George Herbert—an admiration which Bishop, who had cherished Herbert's poetry since she was fourteen, is confident that Moore would share with her.

The ways in which these two poets' interests in Herbert do and do not intersect tell us a good deal about Moore's and Bishop's common values, as well as about their different perspectives on a modernist revaluation of seventeenth-century literature. The subject of their divergent viewpoints I discuss at length in later chapters. In capsule, one might say that Moore's interest in Herbert is that of "the gentlewoman," Bishop's that of "the seeker."[12] That is to say, Moore as devout Christian and moralist is primarily interested in the ethical and emblematic Herbert, just as, I will argue, she is interested in capitalizing on the ethical and emblematic facets of late Renaissance prose. (The Herbert poem that Bishop cites in her 1977 talk on poetic influences as one of Moore's favorites is "Hope," a somewhat cryptic emblematic lyric, which requires us to understand that exchanged concrete particulars—an anchor for a watch, an "optick" [telescope] for a prayer book, and so forth—stand for forms of human petition and for the continually frustrating, enigmatically instructive responses to that petition by the abstraction "Hope.")[13] Bishop as secular seeker more highly values the dramatic, psychological, questing and questioning Herbert, just as she was attracted when an undergraduate to seventeenth-century baroque prose writers for their ability "to portray, not a thought, but a mind thinking."[14] (The poem she imitates early in her career and presents near the end of her life in the same talk on influences is Herbert's "Love Unknown," a dramatic and dreamlike account of the process by which an intractable individual spirit is violently refashioned by divine agency, becoming "new, tender, quick.")[15] These individual intersections with Herbert are in keeping with contrasting emphases readers have noticed in Moore's and Bishop's separate bodies of work: on fixity in Moore's case, for example, versus flux in Bishop's, on the establishment of coherence versus the acceptance of contingency, on the timeless present versus the processive—oppositions that to some extent typify generational (modern versus postmodern) as well as temperamental differences.[16]

But a mutual admiration for Herbert's poetry also points, as I have suggested, to Moore's and Bishop's overlapping interests and values. If Bishop was, as I will show in my second chapter, the more powerfully drawn of the two to Herbert by the tug of specific personal nostalgias as well as by her dramatic and psychological propensities, she and Moore still shared a strong affinity for meditative lyrics in general. Both were drawn to Donne and other Metaphysicals as well as to Gerard Manley Hopkins. Herbert, though, as their use of him as a touchstone in literary reviews and essays and as their frequent mention of him throughout their long correspondence makes clear, was more attractive to both Moore and Bishop than any other religious poet: for his hard-won and constantly self-correcting piety; for what Bishop thought of as his "beautifully tactful manners";[17] for his extraordinary formal inventiveness and finish, which Moore termed in a letter to Bishop, "Herbert's impassioned containment";[18] and for what Elizabeth Bishop praised as the unpretentious seventeenth-century pastor's "naturalness of tone."[19] As late in their correspondence as April 4, 1963, Moore replies to a letter in which Bishop has mentioned T. S. Eliot's critical essay on Herbert: "I haven't seen that T. S. Eliot *Herbert*; wish *you* had one."[20] It is evident, then, that George Herbert served over several decades as an important link between these two women. In their view he embodied—religiously, socially, aesthetically—a specific quality that both of them much admired and consistently emulated: humility.

By singling out this quality for attention, I do not mean to set back the clock of Moore and Bishop criticism by suggesting, yet again, that these two powerful poets should be seen merely as unthreateningly "feminine," meek and demure. Like any discussion of literary influences, this book is a story, or a partial story, of patterns of conservatism and radicalism, of literary persistences and resistances. In the case of both poets with whom I am concerned, these familiar patterns are governed by, and production is enabled by, a special sense of humility. For both Moore and Bishop, humility consists not merely of self-effacing modesty (though there is that), but also of a complex and often subtly combative attitude. It is, paradoxically, bound up with both writers' sense of ambition, with their respective efforts to "set," as Ezra Pound put it, "their own inimitable light upon the mountain," to take their inheritance in hand and "make it new."[21]

For Marianne Moore, whose best poems were composed from 1915 to 1945, "humility" was a kind of watchword; and she generally associated this abstract quality with some form of physical protection, as in this mercurial passage from her 1949 essay "Humility, Concentration, and Gusto":

> "With what shall the artist arm himself save with his humility?" Humility, indeed, is armor, for it realizes that it is impossible to be original, in the sense of doing something that has never been thought of before. Originality is in any case a by-product of sincerity; that is to say, of feeling that is honest and accordingly rejects anything that might cloud the impression, such as unnecessary commas, modifying clauses, or delayed predicates. [CPrMM, pp. 420–421]

The same apparently conservative aesthetic credo, together with the same protective association, turns up in Moore's comment for the 1935 book *Trial Balances*, where she introduces three early poems ("The Map," "The Reprimand," and "Three Valentines") by Elizabeth Bishop, now her new friend and protégée:

> One notices the deferences and vigilances in Miss Bishop's writing, and the debt to Donne and Gerard Hopkins. We look at imitation askance; but like the shell which the hermit-crab selects for itself, it has value—the avowed humility, and the protection. . . . We cannot ever be wholly original; we adopt a thought from a group of notes in the song of a bird, from a foreigner's way of pronouncing English, from the weave in a suit of clothes. Our best and newest thoughts about color have been known to past ages. Nevertheless an indebted thing does not interest us, unless there is originality underneath it. [CPrMM, p. 328]

Here we have Moore's belief that creation is always recreation. Beginning with found things, with what she might call "felicitous phenomena," the artist fashions his or her unoriginal new compositions. Both passages affirm also that it is humility, the self-conscious acknowledgment by an author of indebtedness or unoriginality, that paradoxically makes sincere expression or true originality possible. Humility can enable creativity by protecting the artist with a shell or a suit of armor. Moore (provocatively and self-protectively) leaves it to us to decide from what the artist requires protection: from the criticism of those who might accuse him or her of triviality or naiveté; from unguarded or unformalized emotional self-exposure; perhaps from his or her own ego or from unknowing repetition of another's art; from ineffectual or unequipped resistance to some part of the tradition itself. Against all of these external and internal "foes," in my view, both Moore and Bishop defend themselves with their humility, much as Spenser's Red Cross Knight defends himself with the shield of his Christian faith.

Indeed, as their shared admiration for the religious poetry of George Herbert and others suggests, both these poets associated humility with spiritual as well as literary struggle. Moore's work, populated by armored animals and heroes, repeatedly draws on the time-honored emblem of Christian armor—as in "The Pangolin" or in "His Shield," in which Moore, whose brother John Warner was a Presbyterian minister, says of her hero Presbyter John that "His shield/was his humility."[22] Traditional Christianity is at the heart of her project, and (as I explore in my first chapter) she adopts from her Renaissance Protestant sources, and especially from the poetic prose of Sir Thomas Browne, means for celebrating the virtues of vigilance, courage, faith, tenacity, compassion, and hope—as well as the habit, which she then self-consciously modernizes, of patiently deciphering God's Book of Nature.

Elizabeth Bishop's poetry is neither engaged in Christian emblematizing nor infused with sermonic impulses. Yet it is permeated by religious nostalgia and haunted by what she called the "old correspondences" (see her poem "The Bight").[23] Although Bishop, unlike George Herbert, owns an agnostic and skeptical sensibility, she draws on his *The Temple*, using a similar tone of polite understatement to offer a modern-day portrait of similar spiritual striving and strife. In poems such as "The Moose," "At the Fishhouses," or "The Fish," her minutely observant description is conjoined with ecclesiastical or biblical allusion, and associated with feelings of almost religious yearning and wonder.

With their finely etched descriptive lyrics, both Moore and Bishop continue in their very individual ways the nineteenth-century tradition of meditative nature poetry, even as they covertly quarrel with that tradition, resisting particularly what we might call the Romantic male poet's nonhumility—his tendency imaginatively to dominate both nature and woman as nature or natural object.[24] In this way, Moore's poetry, though it persists in traditional Christian interpretation of animals and objects, declines the "dominion" given in Genesis 1:26 "over the fish of the sea, and over the fowl of the air" (and so forth), and finally insists on the natural world's indifference to and independence from all human compulsions to comprehend and contain.

Like Moore in this regard, Bishop takes pains to acknowledge the limits of human power. Her poetry, related to William Wordsworth's both formally and thematically, subtly subverts many of Wordsworth's poetic practices as it ironically undercuts his consoling myth of responsive, nurturing Nature. Bishop often makes her reader feel that however intelligent, inventive, and morally searching it may be, individual human consciousness is hardly, as it is for the Romantic poet, "divine." It is instead more like the "little rented boat" in her poem "The Fish"—a borrowed and haplessly transient vehicle, occasionally illuminated by brief victories, but even then somewhat battered and small.

In relation, then, to the English literary tradition, to issues of spiritual life, and to the natural world, these two writers begin from and maintain a position of humility—if we understand that quality as conducive to innovation as well as imitation, to subversion as well as submission. I have singled out this term, taking my cue from Moore's poetry and prose, because I think that the notion of humility is helpful for keeping in mind Moore's and Bishop's connection, not just with the memorably described animals and objects with which they are associated so easily and so often, but with larger and universal subjects as well.

Meticulous physical description has been pointed to with admiration in both these women's works. While I acknowledge their passion for verisimilitude, as well as Moore's influence on Bishop's developing descriptive capabilities, in the following chapters I inquire also into the ways in which both Moore and Bishop extend and adapt what I will term the "spiritual tradition" of Anglo-American literature—each within her own poetry of psychological reflection, moral and metaphysical inquiry. Like other modernists, Moore and Bishop self-consciously eschewed those nineteenth-century practices that Pound had denounced as "messy," "sentimentalistic," and "mannerish,"[25] and they strove to invent a harder-edged, more objective poetry than that associated with their Victorian and Romantic forebears.[26] They departed, however, from the strictures of early imagism by amplifying description and by allowing room for meditation or reflection. Unlike Eliot and his followers, who turned from nineteenth-century influences to John Donne and to Elizabethan and Jacobean drama, these poets drew, for reasons I investigate later, primarily on less theatrical, less insistently "masculine" and erotically bold models. I am interested here in how each reassesses her inheritance, selecting and making use of different precursors and different literary and spiritual configurations than those that compelled the chief male modernists; in what Moore's and Bishop's choices of literary models indicate about their responses as modern women writers to twentieth-century poetic dilemmas.

My method here is accumulative. That is, I begin in the first two chapters with a detailed discussion of Moore's and Bishop's (non-Eliotic) seventeenth-century influences; Chapters Three and Four then investigate what I take to be these two poets' gender-inflected responses to Romanticism. Finally, Chapter Five speculates further on the particular appeal for these women writers of their Renaissance male models. That chapter articulates as well the ways in which my own observations about Moore's and Bishop's uses of tradition diverge from recent feminist and masculinist critical paradigms for literary influence.

This study does not attempt to be exhaustive: I do not deal with all these authors' poems, nor do I trace all possible literary influences. (In the post-Romantic era, one thinks of Moore's ambivalent appreciation of Swinburne, but affinity for Henry James; of Bishop's early attachment to Hopkins or the urbane accomplishments of Auden, as well as her complex relation to the poetic project of Wallace Stevens and her exchanges with her friend Robert Lowell.) I have chosen rather to begin the discussion of what I take to be the most significant premodern influences on these poets through readings of what I take to be some of their "best and newest" poems. In doing so I have tried to bring to their verses some of that assiduous attention and capacity for appreciation which (as their correspondence with one another as well as their other writings show) they lavished on literary contemporaries and predecessors alike. How did these two modern women writers, with the help of certain literary kinships or, as Moore put it, "consanguinities," adapt and revise the predominantly male-authored tradition in which they were so well versed? What convictions and obsessions helped to form their two extraordinary bodies of work, which remain (to borrow the title of Moore's early *Trial Balances* piece on Elizabeth Bishop) "archaically new?"

1 ·

"To explain grace requires a curious hand":
Marianne Moore and Seventeenth-Century Prose

ANYONE RIFFLING THROUGH PAGES of the old magazine *The Dial* can see how often Marianne Moore praised and appraised writers of all periods in terms of the seventeenth century. First as a contributor of essays and reviews, and then (after succeeding Scofield Thayer) in her editorial column "Comments," from 1925 to 1929, Moore compared the most unlikely figures. Here, for example, she likens Gertrude Stein's achievement in *The Making of Americans* to John Bunyan's in *The Pilgrim's Progress*: "As Bunyan's Christian is English yet universal, this sober, tender-hearted, very searching history of a family's progress, comprehends in its picture of life which is distinctively American, a psychology which is universal" (CPrMM, p. 131).

Here, a new edition of Boswell's *Life of Johnson* leads her to compare Dr. Johnson's prose style to that of Sir Thomas Browne: "In its remoteness of fashion, the style of this passage recalls Sir Thomas Browne. And in 'the uniform vivid texture' of other of his [Johnson's] prose, surely it is not a mistake to perceive that 'subtlety of disquisition and strength of language' which he found in the author of *The Religio*" (CPrMM, p. 164).

It is Browne she thinks of in her anxiousness to defend Thomas Hardy against charges of pessimism. Her comment on Hardy begins: "Certain of his contemporaries found it upon their consciences to wonder whether Sir Thomas Browne were or were not an atheist" (CPrMM, p. 131). Again, reviewing a new book on speech and grammar, she invokes five exemplary authors, and the seventeenth century walks away with the honors: "We attribute to let us say Machiavelli, Sir Francis Bacon, John Donne, Sir Thomas Browne, Doctor Samuel Johnson, a particular kind of verbal effectiveness—a nicety and point, a pride and pith of utterance, which is in a special way different from the admirableness of Wordsworth or of Hawthorne" (CPrMM, p. 165).

Some of Moore's *Dial* pieces are written directly in praise of seventeenth-century figures, such as her essay on Sir Francis Bacon whose " 'exact diligence' and pleasing defiances," she says, "anticipated not only the mind of close successors, but of our own age" (CPrMM, p. 98). And her last comment as editor of the discontinuing *The Dial* in June 1929—ostensibly a review of one book on the seventeenth century's broadsides and another on its "quacks"—is in fact a celebration of her favorite century:

> Bravura as one of the attributes of the 17th century keeps rising into our vision from time to time like the bouquet of a fountain, its gaudy phrases less richly than the more shadowy ones in Jeremy Taylor, Richard Hooker, or Sir Thomas Browne. . . . 17th century portraits, heraldic emblems carved in the pavements and the little tabernacles within tabernacles in the aisles of cathedral churches, seem to extenuate superficialities of the age, and there were others besides Sir Thomas Browne to whom ashes were more than dust. [CPrMM, p. 221]

Exiting, Moore reminds her *Dial* readers in this final comment's concluding sentence that "the 17th century bears scrutiny." What she has seen there—and particularly in the work of her favorite seventeenth-century figure, Sir Thomas Browne (1605–1682)—is a Christian religious sensibility, a special "pride and pith of utterance," and a general quality of zesty inquiry and boldness. It is a version of the set of values expressed in the title of Moore's famous essay, "Humility, Concentration, and Gusto" (CPrMM, pp. 420–427).

Other readers of Moore have mentioned her admiration for the range of seventeenth-century writers—Bacon, Hooker, Greville, Raleigh, Jeremy Taylor, Burton, Milton and Clarendon—whom she had studied in a 1909 course entitled "Imitative Writing" as a student at Bryn Mawr.[1] (Book Five of Browne's *Urn Burial*, together with some essays by Francis Bacon, was on Moore's Bryn Mawr reading list as early as her sophomore year, 1906-1907.)[2] In a *Dial* review of Moore's landmark second book, *Observations* (1924), Glenway Wescott noted: "The prototype of Miss Moore's 'observations' is the Baconian essay, or the prose of Sir Thomas Browne or Burton."[3] And Louise Bogan put the case for this connection most forcefully in a brief 1947 essay, stating that Marianne Moore "does not resemble certain seventeenth-century writers; she might be one of them."[4] No one, however, has yet taken up in a more thoroughgoing manner the subject of the concerns and stylistic "predilections" (to borrow one of Moore's favorite words) that this modernist adapted from her late Renaissance sources.

Such an inquiry might help us to see more clearly how Moore's poems are made and what her unique project as an American modernist was. A great part of Moore's distinction from other modern American poets lies in the fact that her poetry enacts a sort of nervous marriage of certain Renaissance prose subjects and strategies with modernist "objectivism" and linguistic self-consciousness.[5] Or perhaps it would be more true to say that we sense in her work not so much a marriage as a tension or torsion of Renaissance and modernist forces. Her best poems might be said to "work" in the manner of mechanical clocks that keep time accurately because they have been tightly wound.

Like the anteater with imbricated scales which is the subject of "The Pangolin," Moore's writing is "strongly intailed, neat," and so exemplifies that "charm of neatness" that Ezra Pound praised in *The Spirit of Romance*.[6] Again like her pangolin ("Pangolins . . . are models of exactness"), her work embodies what Pound elsewhere called the "touchstone" of "precision."[7] It is a rather dry and prosy poetry (approved of by Pound for its "arid clarity"),[8] insistently factual and tending toward natural history:

> Armor seems extra. But for him,
> the closing ear-ridge—
> or bare ear lacking even this small
> eminence and similarly safe
>
> contracting nose and eye apertures
> impenetrably closable, are not. . . .

Neither headily musical nor dreamily nostalgic, this is writing emphatically non-Keatsian and non-Pre-Raphaelite: modern. Yet Moore's interest in exotic objects or animals, her unusual linguistic and syntactic practices, and her consistent emphasis on religious as well as naturalistic and aesthetic "grace" (the word appears seven times in "The Pangolin") show her close kinship with the seventeenth-century predecessors she admired.

Prose writers of that century, for instance, were eager to take the "brave new world" and the new science into their sentences. Moore is like them (and like the extensive, encompassing glacier of her poem "An Octopus") in her enormous "capacity for fact." Like them, she conjoins scientific inquiry with a kooky delight in the strange. Bonnie Costello has called Moore a "kleptomaniac of the mind," a phrase which the poet undoubtedly would have relished and jotted down in one of her numerous notebooks.[9] A great collector of phrases, quaint lore, even odd objects—keeping in her small Brooklyn apartment a paper nautilus, mechanical crow and elephant, Chinese brass lizard, green bronze lizard, teak mouse, rat with carnelian eyes, pickled coral snake and fly-shaped chunk of amber with a fly in it (CPrMM, p. 688)[10]—Moore admired whatever seemed "new and strange" in the work of others, enjoying, for example, Wallace Stevens's flavor of eclectic exoticism. As she says: "One is excited by the sense of proximity to Java peacocks, golden pheasants, South American macaw feather capes, Chilcat blankets, hair seal needlework, Singalese masks, and Rousseau's paintings of banana leaves and alligators" (CPrMM, p. 92).

But Moore's own use of the exotic has more in common with her much older predecessors than with her contemporary. She does not share the pagan vision of Wallace Stevens:

> Supple and turbulent, a ring of men
> Shall chant in orgy on a summer morn
> Their boisterous devotion to the sun,
> Not as a god, but as a god might be,
> Naked among them, like a savage source.[11]

In her poetics there is a place for the "cockatoo/Upon a rug," but not for this boisterous heresy. Her world is not "an old chaos of the sun." She continues to see the sun as emblematic of God, and her poetry can still, like Donne's or Herbert's, make that Christian pun—as here in the concluding lines of "The Pangolin":

> "Again the sun!
>   anew each day; and new and new and new,
>   that comes into and steadies my soul."

Or in these more difficult lines, which I take to be at least partially about divine judgment, from "Sun":

> O Sun, you shall stay
> with us; holiday,

        consuming wrath, be wound in a device
     of Moorish gorgeousness, round glasses spun
    to flame as hemispheres of one
great hour-glass dwindling to a stem. Consume hostility;
employ your weapon in this meeting-place of surging
    enmity!
     Insurgent feet shall not outrun
     multiplied flames, O Sun.

(This is the second half of a two-part poem reminiscent of the seventeenth century in another way as well: printed to resemble the hourglass it describes, it is a "shaped" poem in the tradition of George Herbert's "The Altar" or "Easter Wings." And possibly the "Moorish" is a pun, a Donne-ish gesture.)

Moore's collector's approach is very much in the tradition of late sixteenth- and early seventeenth-century prodigious troves, such as Walter Cope's "wonder-cabinet," which was said to include an embalmed child, a unicorn's tail, a flying rhinoceros, and a sea mouse[12]—or of Sir Thomas Browne's amassment "of the eggs of all the fowl and birds he could procure."[13] And her oeuvre to some extent resembles such literary miscellanies as Browne's 1646 *Pseudodoxia Epidemica* (*Vulgar Errors*), which itself stands in self-consciously belated relation to earlier and more credulous works such as Edward Topsell's 1607 *Historie of Foure-Footed Beastes* (translated and adapted from Conrad Gesner's *Historiae Animalium*). Like these late Renaissance writers—and unlike the author of "Sunday Morning"—Moore shows a sense of religious purpose in her celebration, and symbolical interpretation, of the plenitude of creation.

Edward Topsell (1572–1625) concludes his *Historie*—a compilation of information about unusual animals, including the elephant, the rhinoceros, the unicorn, and a beast called the "tatus or Guinean," which is an armored animal like Moore's pangolin—with an admonishing Epilogue: "Therefore (well minded Readers) herein you shall satisfie your own consciences and harts, when the visible things of the world, doe lead you to the invisible things of God, and all these rowes and ranks of living Four-Footed Beasts are as letters and Mid-wives to save the reverence which is due to the highest (that made them) from perishing within you."[14] Moore had certainly read Edward Topsell by 1927 when she quoted him in her editorial comment "On Serpents" ("As Edward Topsell has said in his *Historie of Serpents*, 'Among all kinds of serpents there is none comparable to the Dragon'" [CPrMM, p. 187]). And I think it probable she had already read him by 1925, and so shared in editor Scofield Thayer's little joke when he "rebuked" her (as that year's *Dial* award winner) for not having taken Topsell into account in the notes to her poem "Sea Unicorns"—Topsell having soberly questioned the absolute authority of the fable that Moore's poem promulgates, that only virgins can tame unicorns.[15] The "kleptomaniac of the mind" and the seventeenth-century minister and compiler of naturalistic description, medicinal advice, mythological lore, and religious interpretation are in some ways kindred spirits, and were surely felt to be so by Moore. In Moore as in Topsell—although of course with more poetry, humor, and modernist self-consciousness on her part—we find the interplay of general curiosity, rational inquiry, and traditional Christian piety.

In "The Jerboa," as in so many of Moore's poems, her separate attractions to visible things and to invisible meanings intriguingly compete. The poem begins with a description of an enormous bronze "cone—pine cone/or fir cone—with holes for a fountain," which was designed for a Roman and "passed/for art." Then the poem proceeds to "collect" Egyptian curiosities:

> These people liked small things;
> they gave to boys little paired playthings such as
>   nests of eggs, ichneumon and snake, paddle
>   and raft, badger and camel;

and made toys for them-
selves: the royal totem;
    and toilet boxes marked
    with the contents. Lords and ladies put goose-grease
        paint in round bone boxes—the pivoting
        lid incised with a duck-wing

Both the Roman pinecone and the Egyptian artifacts, the "huge cast bronze" and the "small things," are examples, as the subtitle of this section tells us, of "Too Much"; and lest we forget the message in our attention to all these interesting items, Moore concludes this first part with a summarizing moral: "but one would not be he/who has nothing but plenty." It is almost a rebuke to her own (and to her engrossed reader's) rapt absorption in multiplicity and detail.

The second section of this same poem, entitled "Abundance," consists mostly of Moore's description of the jerboa, a small desert rat—a description similar to, but more deft and musical than, the sort one might find in the *Natural History* articles this poet habitually read:

Looked at by daylight,
the underside's white,
    though the fur on the back
    is buff-brown like the breast of the fawn-breasted
        bower-bird. It hops like the fawn-breast, but has
        chipmunk contours—perceived as

it turns its bird head—
the nap directed
    neatly back and blending
    with the ear which reiterates the slimness
        of the body. . . .

There are reminders in this half of the poem as well that what is described so meticulously in these partially rhymed stanzas possesses some further moral significance. Moore likens the jerboa to Jacob, reminding us that the drab country it inhabits is also associated with Scripture and with proximity to God:

> Part terrestrial,
> and part celestial,
>> Jacob saw, cudgel staff
>> in claw-hand—steps of air and air angels; his
>>> friends were the stones. . . .

By the end of the poem, the small rodent, like so many of Moore's creatures, comes to embody, minutely, alertness to danger, humility, and an attractive efficiency like that of functional art:

>   . . . It
> honors the sand by assuming its color;
>> closed upper paws seeming one with the fur
>> in its flight from danger.
>
> . . . .
>
> Its leaps should be set
> to the flageolet;
>> pillar body erect
>> on a three-cornered smooth-working Chippendale
>>> claw—propped on hind legs, and tail as third toe,
>>> between leaps to its burrow.

The overt moral point of this poem, which concludes with this simultaneously ridiculous and stately portrait of the desert rat, is that simplicity is superior to luxury—the theme of luxury being picked up in the next poem in *The Complete Poems*, "Camellia Sabina." But if we look at the poem in the context of Moore's work as a whole, we see that "The Jerboa" also offers a variation on her recurrent theme of Christian courage; in Topsellian terms, "the visible things of the world" lead her "to the invisible things of God." The little animal's alertness to danger and capacity for expeditious action may be found as well in the "heroes" of other poems, such as "The Hero," "The Frigate Pelican," and

"The Pangolin." Moore implies, for example, that the pro-
tagonist of "The Hero" does finally act in the face of unnerving fears, even though he shares the anxieties and timidities
of ordinary persons like ourselves:

> We do not like some things, and the hero
>   doesn't; deviating headstones
>   and uncertainty;
>   going where one does not wish
>   to go; suffering and not
>   saying so; standing and listening where something
>   is hiding. The hero shrinks
> as what it is flies out on muffled wings, with twin yellow
> eyes—to and fro—

The way to surmount fear, Moore makes us believe in this
poem, is to proceed "like Pilgrim," by means of a stalwart
brand of hope that sounds very much like Christian faith
("hope not being hope/until all ground for hope has/
vanished"). Similarly, the frigate pelican overcomes dangerous fatigue, which arrives in the form of a python (an
uncharacteristically unappealing serpent for Moore, here
evocative of Satan or of the temptation to despair):

> But he, and others, soon

> rise from the bough and though flying, are able to foil the
>   tired
>   moment of danger that lays on heart and lungs the
>   weight of the python that crushes to powder.

And the "serge-clad, strong-shod" representative of humanity who is likened by Moore to her pangolin sur-
mounts his fears by addressing the sun (or "Son" of God):

> . . . The prey of fear, he, always
>   curtailed, extinguished, thwarted by the dusk, work
>   partly done,
> says to the alternating blaze,
>   "Again the sun!
>   anew each day; and new and new and new,
>   that comes into and steadies my soul."

Obviously, words such as *danger* and *hope* are freighted with Christian significance in Moore's work. Danger is consistently aligned with the threat of darkness, fatigue, and despair (the loss of faith that Renaissance writers called "wanhope"), while "hope" is associated with light (the sun, or "Son"), fortitude, and salvation. In short, Moore's recurrent themes show her to be a devotional poet in the tradition of Fulke Greville, John Donne, and George Herbert—even though her work generally lacks the sense of introspection and psychological struggle that we find in Greville's "In night, when colors all to black are cast," Donne's "Batter my heart," or Herbert's "Affliction" poems. These seventeenth-century poets achieve, by means of psychological intensity, a complexity that keeps their verses from being merely clever expressions of easy pieties. Moore avoids the same pitfall by involving us not so much in the process of introspection as in physical observation of and moral observations about the richly diverse world outside herself. Much of the energy in her poems comes from this interfusion of the interests of the naturalist and the devout Christian; for Moore, as for Edward Topsell, it is crucial to show how "Science is Divine."

Moore, who never married, was extraordinarily close to her religiously devout mother (with whom she lived until the latter died when Marianne was sixty) and to her Presbyterian minister brother, John Warner, to whom she wrote frequently, often with suggestions for sermons.[16] She showed her poems to both of them, soliciting their—and particularly Mrs. Moore's—advice. Mrs. Moore's father too had been a Presbyterian minister, and it seems likely that the family thought of itself as engaged in a common endeavor "to explain grace" ("The Pangolin"), and that Moore conceived of her own poetry as complementary to her brother's vocation. The study of nature for Moore is a religious act, akin to biblical exegesis. Her employment of natural history for devotional purposes is in accordance with the notion of God's "two books," a Renaissance commonplace that Topsell invokes in the "Dedicatory" to his *Historie of Foure-Footed Beastes:* "For how shall we be able to speak the whole Counsell of God unto his people, if we read unto them but one of his bookes, when he hath another in the worlde, which wee never study past the title or outside; although the great God have made them an Epistle Dedicatory to the whole race of mankind." Sir Thomas Browne reiterates the idea in his 1643 *Religio Medici (The Religion of a Physician)*: "Thus there are two bookes from which I collect my Divinity; besides that written one of God, another of his servant Nature, that universall and publik Manuscript, that lies expans'd unto the Eyes of all."[17]

Although Moore quotes from a wide variety of seventeenth-century devotional literature in her poetry and prose (Lancelot Andrewes' sermons, Jeremy Taylor's devotional manuals, Richard Baxter's *The Saint's Everlasting Rest,* and the Authorized Version of the Bible), it is Browne who is, as her own critical writings evince, the seventeenth-century figure closest to her own heart. It is not difficult to imagine Moore and Browne comfortably conversing—so much do they speak in the same terms, symbols, and even cadences. Moore had never seen her father, John Milton Moore, who had been institutionalized before her birth after he suffered a nervous breakdown. She seems to have found a sort of spiritual father in the seventeenth-century physician and author of *Religio Medici; Pseudodoxia Epidemica; Hydriotaphia, Urn-Burial; The Garden of Cyrus;* and *Christian Morals.*

Known for his affectionate, advisory letters to his eldest son Edward (who also became a doctor) and to his second son Thomas (who was in the navy), which were found among his papers and published with his collected *Works,* Browne was a devoted father. And in other ways as well he must have seemed to Moore both attractive and exemplary. Browne promulgated, on the whole, humane and latitudinarian Christian views.[18] Although his *Religio Me-*

dici was placed on the Catholic Index of Prohibited Books in 1645, and although he was accused of atheism by more militant fellow Protestant contemporaries, Browne managed to live an irenic, prosperous, and well-respected long life in the city of Norwich—recognized as the leading expert on flora and fauna in Norfolk and Suffolk, and knighted as his city's most distinguished citizen by Charles II in 1671.[19] One might say of this productive and inquisitive private citizen, who successfully survived England's Civil War and deflected dangerous charges of impiety, that "his shield/was his humility" (see Moore's poem, "His Shield"). Browne's cautious presentation of his *Religio* in that book's forward as merely "private exercise directed to my self," his canny demurral there that "there are many things delivered Rhetorically, many expressions meerely Tropicall [i.e., merely figurative]," and his extensive citation throughout his work of ecclesiastical and classical authorities were evidently efficient defensive strategies, which seem to have been duly noted and adapted for her own situation by the well-armored modern poet. Moore herself modestly scrupled to put forth her own work as "poetry,"[20] employed wily and ambiguous figurative language, and peppered her work idiosyncratically with sometimes unambiguously authoritative, sometimes ironically positioned quotations.

Certainly, Moore's *Complete Poems* appear playfully indebted to Browne's literary menagerie, *Pseudodoxia Epidemica*, when we compare his table of contents to her own. Browne's entries, for example, include "Of the Elephant," "Of the Basilisk," "Of Snayles," "Of the Chameleon," "Of the Unicorn's horn," and a note on a "popular and received tenet" that "the Ostridge digesteth Iron"—while Moore writes poems entitled "Elephants," "The Plumet Basilisk," "To a Snail," "To a Chameleon," "Sea Unicorns and Land Unicorns," and a poem about the ostrich called "He 'Digesteth Hard Yron'."

And there are other striking similarities, large and small,

between Browne's prose and Moore's poetry. Moore encountered in Browne that Topsellian insistence on the emblematic nature of the physical world which she herself would also voice in "He 'Digesteth Hard Yron' " ("the power of the visible/is the invisible"). Here is Browne in his *Religio*: "The severe Schooles shall never laugh me out of the Philosophy of *Hermes*, that this visible world is but a picture of the invisible, wherein as in a pourtract, things are not truely, but in equivocall shapes, and as they counterfeit some reall substance in that invisible fabrick" (I, 21).

The poet who had been trained in biology at Bryn Mawr and who made precise, witty drawings of so many nonhuman creatures (for example, a baby opossum, jerboas, a tiger salamander, a sleeping leopard, a katydid)[21] found in the *Religio* a consanguine regard for the study of animals as an act of religious devotion:

> The world was made to be inhabited by beasts, but studied and contemplated by man: 'tis the debt of our reason wee owe unto God, and the homage wee pay for not being beasts; without this the world is still as though it had not been, or as it was before the sixth day, when as yet there was not a creature that could conceive, or say there was a world. The wisedome of God receives small honour from those vulgar heads, that rudely stare about, and with a grosse rusticity admire his works; those highly magnifie him, whose judicious enquiry into his acts, and deliberate research of his creatures, return the duty of a devout and learned admiration. [I, 22]

And she found in Browne's book a congenial admiration for even unlikely, "unlovely" animals as also God's art: "I hold there is a general beauty in [all] the works of God, and therefore no deformity in any kind or species of creature whatsoever. I cannot tell by what Logick we call a Toad, a Beare, or an Elephant, ugly; they being created in those outward shapes and figures which best express the actions of their inward formes" (I, 26).

The elephant, specifically mentioned here by Browne,

who also argues in his *Pseudodoxia Epidemica* against the "vulgar error" or common belief that the elephant has no joints, is one subject especially favored by Moore. In "The Monkeys" she admiringly and accurately observes "the elephants with their fog-colored skin/and strictly practical appendages." In "Elephants" she portrays, with almost surreal specificity, two beasts with intertwined trunks— and creates in the process a sort of self-parody of excessive modification:

> Uplifted and waved till immobilized
> wistaria-like, the opposing opposed
> mouse-gray twined proboscises' trunk formed by two
> trunks, fights itself to a spiraled inter-nosed
>
> deadlock of dyke-enforced massiveness. . . .

And in "Black Earth" (a fine early poem, later entitled "Melancthon," which she unfortunately dropped from her collections after her 1951 *Collected Poems*), Moore presents the battered elephant with its thick skin, "cut into checkers by rut/upon rut of unpreventable experience," as a symbol of spiritual beauty and endurance: "My soul," the creature staunchly says, as the poet's alter ego, "shall never be cut into/by a wooden spear."[22]

Moore and her seventeenth-century "father" even attribute the same significances to specific physical phenomena. In the fourth book of *Pseudodoxia Epidemica*, for example— after some discussion of "proneness" and erectness in such creatures as frogs, oxen, and birds—Browne links physically upright stature with the capacity for spiritual striving and understanding ("Only *Man* hath an erect figure, and for to behold and look up toward heaven" [II, 269]). And this idea (a purely *figurative* notion, as Browne insists, originating with Plato) corresponds with Moore's symbolic use of this trait in such poems as "The Jerboa," "Pedantic Literalist," "The Fish," and "What Are Years?." We see the jerboa escaping danger (i.e., despair or loss of faith) by bounding to its burrow, standing between leaps with "pillar body erect." The literalist "with the perfunctory heart" is rebuked for his lack of spirit by the poet who says, "what stood/erect in you has withered." The scarred and admirable cliff in "The Fish" (reminiscent of the battered elephant in "Black Earth") erectly withstands mere physical assault:

> All
> external
> > marks of abuse are present on this
> > defiant edifice—
> > > all the physical features of
>
> ac-
> cident—lack
> > of cornice, dynamite grooves, burns, and
> > hatchet strokes, these things stand
> > > out on it; the chasm side is
>
> dead.
> Repeated
> > evidence has proved that it can live
> > on what cannot revive
> > > its youth. The sea grows old in it.

And the upright bird in the concluding stanza of the stirring, unabashedly sermonic "What Are Years?" is yet another emblem of spiritual stamina and survival:

> So he who strongly feels,
> behaves. The very bird,
> > grown taller as he sings, steels
> his form straight up. Though he is captive,
> his mighty singing
> says, satisfaction is a lowly
> thing, how pure a thing is joy.
> > This is mortality,
> > this is eternity.

(Birds are the creatures Browne singles out in the *Pseudodoxia* as "almost Erect" [II, 270]; and in his *Religio* he also remarks, "the way to be immortall is to die daily." [I, 55]).

Finally, in "The Pangolin," when Moore turns from the anteater as her ostensible subject to "man"—in all his ridiculousness and nobility, his potential for failure and for grace—she marks the turn by describing the pangolin as standing "on hind feet plantigrade,/with certain postures of a man." (The recondite "plantigrade" here keeps the poem characteristically anchored in scientific diction and physical fact, while at the same time calling attention to Moore's moral theme.)

Browne takes a human trait, erect stature, and grants it spiritual significance; Moore then endows her nonhuman subjects with this symbolized feature. Moore's subjects— the jerboa, the cliff, the bird, the pangolin—do possess, in some degree, the quality of physical erectness, though they do not of course possess human spirits. As a result, Moore's description in these poems hovers between the factual and the metaphorical, the scientific and the symbolic. Her method ensures that she is "not untrue" (to borrow Moore's distinctive trope of litotes) to either the visible or the invisible world.

In her poems about amphibious creatures (these include the salamander, the chameleon, the dragon, and the basilisk), Moore once again elaborates on a physical trait that has for her the same symbolic value it has for Browne, who writes in his *Religio*:

> We are onely that amphibious piece between a corporall and spirituall essence, that middle frame that links those two together, and makes good the method of God and nature. . . . thus is man that great and true *Amphibium*, whose nature is disposed to live not onely like other creatures in divers elements, but in divided and distinguished worlds: for though there bee but one [world] to the sense, there are two to reason; the one visible; the other invisible. [I, 44–45]

For Moore, who reminds us in a 1965 *Harper's Bazaar* piece that "amphi" means "both" (CPrMM, p. 573), amphibiousness becomes a metaphor for man's—and in "The

Pangolin," of course, she follows Browne in using that noun generically—uniquely double position in creation. Because he is a creature like others, man inhabits the visible world with its "divers elements"; because he is the *rational* creature, he also inhabits that other, invisible world. Just as she evokes the human capacity for spiritual endurance by describing erect objects or animals, Moore at times evokes humankind's dual nature by describing amphibious animals.

In her most ambitious poem in this mode, Moore describes "The Plumet Basilisk," an "amphibious falling dragon," as "the ruler of Rivers, Lakes, and Seas,/invisible or visible." It is also a creature capable of a sort of rebirth:

> he is alive there
>   in his basilisk cocoon beneath
> the one of living green; his quicksilver ferocity
>   quenched in the rustle of his fall into the sheath
> which is the shattering sudden splash that marks his
>   temporary loss.

"To a Chameleon," from Moore's 1958 book *O To Be a Dragon*, similarly suggests the human capacity for spiritual survival—especially if we keep in mind Moore's repeated equation of physical protection with Christian salvation in such poems as "The Pangolin," "Armor's Undermining Modesty," and "His Shield." The chameleon's camouflaged invisibility is associated with protection as well as with great beauty: the jewel-like chameleon's changeable coloration keeps it "Hid by the august foliage and fruit of the grape-vine." (The twining form of this poem, again in the seventeenth-century emblematic tradition, imitates on the page the chameleon's posture around the grapevine.)

What we see in these poems is Moore's adaptation for her own purposes of the metaphor espoused by Browne. His attention is on man; Moore develops the other half of the figure, describing amphibious animals in a manner that evokes man's capacity for both mortal and immortal existence. In this way, Moore exercises her "capacity for fact" while insisting upon her Christian concerns. It is as if it were her poetic project to be the dragon "of silkworm/size or immense; at times invisible." She wants to stay in touch with the smallest concrete details (the snail's "occipital horn"), while remaining attentive to the largest abstract truths.

From her most important seventeenth-century predecessor, Moore adopts, too, some specific points of style. Marie Borroff, whom Harold Bloom has called "the best reader of the language of Moore's language,"[23] has argued, through meticulous stylistic analysis, for the likeness of Moore's poetry to "promotional prose."[24] Nevertheless, most of the salient features that Borroff catalogues in Moore's poems and compares to features found in magazine and newspaper articles or advertisements appear also with marked frequency in the poetic prose of Sir Thomas Browne. Here, for example, is a brief (amused and amusing) passage from the *Pseudodoxia*, which exhibits four main features from Borroff's list—Latinate diction, elaborate syntax, terms of negation, and the citation of authority:[25] "That some Elephants have not only written whole sentences, as AElian ocularly testifieth, but have also spoken, as Oppianus delivereth, and Christophorus a Costa particularly relateth; although it sounds like that of Achilles' Horse in Homer, we do not conceive impossible" (II, 161). (Here we may be reminded also of a different sort of *tonal* feature Browne shares with the modern poet, who wrote in "The Pangolin" that "humor saves a few steps, it saves years.") We find too in Browne's *Pseudodoxia* and in other late Renaissance writing the scientific terminology that Borroff claims for Moore's likeness to promotional prose. The term "proboscis," for one example, enters English in the late sixteenth century; "amphibious" comes into the language in the seventeenth century, as do "aperture" and the fancy "bedizened" that bedeck "The Pangolin." And characterizing both Moore and her information-dense seventeenth-century model are participial constructions. Here, from the *Pseudodoxia*: "Many Opinions are passant *concerning* the Basilisk or little King of Serpents, commonly called the Cockatrice: some *affirming*, others *denying*, most *doubting* the relations made hereof" (II, 174, my emphases). And from Moore's "An Octopus":

> The Greeks liked smoothness, *distrusting* what was back
> of what could not be clearly seen,
> *resolving* with benevolent conclusiveness,
> "complexities which still will be complexities
> as long as the world lasts";
> *ascribing* what we clumsily call happiness,
> to "an accident or a quality, . . ."
>
> [my emphases]

Finally, Browne's prose, like Moore's poetry, is replete with words that Marie Borroff calls "stative" rather than "dynamic"—nouns and verbs that point to permanent and absolute concepts rather than temporary and variable ones. Both writers, for instance, characteristically use the stative verb "to be" (which does also appear, of course, in aggressive feature writing and advertising):

> The heart of man is the place the Devils dwell in.
> thus is Man that great and true Amphibium
> there is a general beauty in the works of God
> the way to be immortal is to die daily
>
> (SIR THOMAS BROWNE)

> Love/is the only fortress/strong enough to trust to.
> Truth is no Apollo/Belvedere, no formal thing.
> The power of the visible/is the invisible;
> This is mortality,/this is eternity.
>
> (MARIANNE MOORE)

Borroff herself suggests that the quality most distinguishing Moore's poetry from popular periodical writing is its thematic emphasis on a "Platonic unity underlying diversity, a One manifest in the many";[26] and indeed these last quotations are reminders that Moore and her important precursor share a passion for moral absolutes and a devotion to the "one" God manifest in His creations, which is difficult to find in promotional prose.

Ingeniously, Borroff has versified the following prose passage from a 1930 Swedish Travel Bureau advertisement; it "not only looks," she says, "but sounds like a stanza from a poem by Marianne Moore":[27]

> There's a girl who might
>   have stepped out of the sixteenth century:
> billowing skirt, gai-
>   ly striped apron, tight
>   black bodice . . .
>   they still dress
> like that in Dalecarlia. In their spotless
>   wooden farmhouses you may
> still see the rare old Biblical
>   wall paintings; you may still
>   hear the whirr
> of the shuttle and watch the housewife deftly
>   weaving her
> cloth. You can read by electric light
> and call up London by telephone.

While the manipulated passage does suggest Moore's factual dryness, and does imitate some of her less emphatic line rhythms and unaccentuated rhymes, it does not convey the sense of a fine poet's shifting, apt measures, refusal of prosaic slackness, or surprising syntactic practices. As Borroff herself takes care to remind us, the resemblances of Moore's writing to promotional prose cannot explain the *power* of her poetry: "We could not do without the admixture of eccentricity and originality that perfuses her language: the Latinate technical terms; the polysyllabic rarities and neologisms; the freewheeling images that compare lions' heads to flowers, flowers to the feathers of Andalusian cocks, and the tails of cocks to scimitars; the ellipses and divagations; the sudden flashes of aphorism and satiric wit."[28]

And although the resemblances of Moore's writing to Browne's poetic prose also cannot adequately explain her poetry's unique power, these sentences from the learned and whimsical seventeenth-century physician's *Hydriotaphia, Urn-Burial*, certainly sound more like her:

> Antiquity held too light thoughts from Objects of mortality, while some drew provocatives of mirth from Anatomies, and Juglers shewed tricks with Skeletons. [I, 151]

> What songs the *Syrens* sang, or what name *Achilles* assumed when he hid himself among women, though puzling Questions are not beyond all conjecture. [I, 165]

> But in this latter Scene of time, we cannot expect such Mummies unto our memories, when ambition may fear the Prophecy of *Elias*, and *Charles* the fifth can never hope to live within two *Methusela's* of *Hektor*. [I, 166]

Here we have the love of allusion, the Latinity, the odd compression, sound-stitching, and interesting obliquity of the poet who composed lines like these:

> . . . Though Mars is excessive
>   in being preventive,
> heroes need not write an ordinall of attributes to enumerate
> what they hate.
>   ("ARMOR'S UNDERMINING MODESTY")

Or these:

> that striking grasp of opposites
> opposed each to the other, not to unity,
> which in cycloid inclusiveness
> has dwarfed the demonstration
> of Columbus with the egg—
> a triumph of simplicity—
> that charitive Euroclydon
> of frightening disinterestedness
> which the world hates . . .
>   ("MARRIAGE")

Moore's famous "light rhymes" (first pointed out and named by T. S. Eliot) seem, from this perspective, like the uncovering and displaying of prose felicities: what is buried in Browne ("Antiquity"/"mortality"; "Mummies"/"memories") is dis-covered by Moore's line breaks ("excessive"/ "preventive"; "demonstration"/ "Euroclydon"; "unity"/ "simplicity").[29]

In one stylistic feature, however—the habit of using extended complex noun phrases, often in premodifying position, to compact specifically descriptive information— Moore's writing does more strongly resemble twentieth-century promotional writing. Borroff supplies the following examples from advertisements and articles: "The two long, rodlike, backwardly directed supporting bones of the tongue" and "Cream-in-the-coffee butcher-weave spun rayon dashing buccaneer."[30] Moore's condensed analogies often do syntactically resemble the copywriter's efforts at concreteness (a kylin or "Chinese unicorn," for example, is "long-/tailed or tailless/small cinnamon-brown, common/ camel-haired"; rose thorns are "wide-spaced great/blunt alternating ostrich-skin warts"; a swan has "flamingo-colored, maple-/leaflike feet"). But the terms of Moore's comparisons, as Borroff herself points out, are usually far more innovative and surprising, and less meet, in their bizarreness and refusal of banality, for the advertiser's needs—as her notorious correspondence with the Ford Motor Company proved. Asked to name a new car, Moore proposed (and here I reproduce her capitalization and spelling) the terrifically improbable "MONGOOSE CIVIQUE," "PASTELOGRAM," "pluma piluma," "andante con moto," and "UTOPIAN TURTLETOP."[31] (Finally the company gave up, sent Moore roses, and named the car Edsel.)

This extreme fancifulness in Moore has been discussed by Robert Pinsky in *The Situation of Poetry*. He cites as an example of Moore's "dandyism" her description of fir

trees in "A Grave" ("each with an emerald turkey-foot at
the top")—and he sees Moore's self-conscious descriptive
techniques (as well as Wallace Stevens's techniques) as a
response to the modern poet's dilemma: believing (or
suspecting) that there are "no ideas but in *things*," while
being inescapably committed to the expression of ideas in
words, which are abstractions. According to Pinsky's account of this modernist dilemma, the "oddball image or
analogy" amounts to a kind of nervous compromise, "a
sort of stylistic diffident cough, a self-effacing exaggera-
tion of gesture. By means of it, the poet indicates both his
wish to vanish in favor of the object, and his inability to
do so."[32] Moore's elaborate, often unlikely comparisons,
then, may be seen as a mark of her self-conscious modernity. Surely, such compressed metaphors and similes account for many moments of pleasure in her poems: a cat
has "a prune-shaped head/and alligator-eyes"; a pangolin
is an "ant- and stone-swallowing uninjurable/artichoke";
a waterfall is "an endless skein swayed by the wind"; an
elephant, "black earth preceded by a tendril." Virtuoso
analogies (which serve to refresh and desolemnize poems
that might otherwise be oppressively moralistic) point *out*
to the world of things, even as they point *back* to the poet
as self-conscious source.

Still, Moore's complex descriptive strategies may also
be seen as traditional. Her meticulous physical observation leads to moral observation, as we have seen;
and she is capable of employing abstract terms such as
"hope," "love," "humility," and "grace" without excuse
or undermining irony. As Bonnie Costello says, "Moore
approaches the process of analogy with a special self-
consciousness that marks her as 'modern' "; yet, as Costello also acknowledges: "Moore's poems enter into a
long and varied tradition of emblematic literature in which
images are juxtaposed to ideas or morals with which they
have little natural but primarily an abstract connection."[33]
Or we could find another astute summary in Elizabeth

Bishop's "Invitation to Miss Marianne Moore," in which she praised her older friend's work in phrases that might describe Thomas Browne's work as well. Both the modern and the seventeenth-century writer compose sentences "with dynasties of negative constructions/darkening and dying . . . /With grammar that suddenly turns and shines/ like flocks of sandpipers flying"; for both, the world is "all awash with morals."

Moore's uniquely complex, usually syllabically determined stanzaic patterns point to her simultaneous modernity and traditionalism—reminding us of the formal inventiveness of Donne and Herbert, even as they display daring line breaks and word breaks ("ac/cident"; "and so/ on"; "cautious-/ly") that the radical William Carlos Williams could admire: "Miss Moore gets great pleasure from wiping soiled words or cutting them clean out, removing the aureoles that have been pasted about them or taking them bodily from greasy contexts. . . . With Miss Moore a word is a word most when it is separated out by science, treated with acid to remove the smudges, washed, dried, and placed right side up on a clean surface."[34] (Unsurprisingly, what Williams admires most in Moore's work is its resemblance to his own. Even the doctor's metaphors here—surgeon and laboratory scientist—suggest his projection of his own project upon hers. Williams sees Moore's crisp linguistic manipulations and scientific exactitude. What he does not see is the devotional poet and Christian moralist so unlike himself; he even compliments Moore on "a very welcome and not little surprising absence of moral tone.")[35]

The major American poets of Moore's generation—Williams, of course, among them—wanted above all to "make it new." In order, though, to realize Pound's well-known injunction, the poet must have some sense of the literary tradition; he or she must have some idea of what the "it" is. A writer cannot afford to be unaware of his or her inheritance, since such unconsciousness results, as

Robert Pinsky points out, in a "lapse into mere mannerism or received ideas."[36] Williams attempted to free himself as an American writer by jettisoning as much convention as possible (although the *total* abandonment of convention in literature is, of course, an impossibility), while Moore selectively adopted—and adapted—inherited attitudes and techniques. Some of Moore's poems, perhaps especially some late ones, may be mannered or coy, but her best poems (among these "The Steeple-Jack," "A Grave," "The Fish," "Marriage," "An Octopus," "Virginia Britannia," and "The Pangolin") do not "lapse." Rather, they show clearly that quality she herself admired in other artists—a "capacity for newness inclusive of oldness" (CPrMM, p. 204).

"To explain grace requires a curious hand," Moore writes in "The Pangolin"—and in this phrase I think she describes her own project and gives us a clue to her procedures. Her work, which includes literary-critical vignettes, meticulous physical descriptions and elevated, psalm-like outbursts, endeavors to set forth clearly or to make intelligible principles of aesthetic, naturalistic, and religious grace. She uses her deep familiarity with late Renaissance prose writing to invent the "curious hand" that her project requires—the word "curious" being etymologically descended from the Latin *cura* and related to the English "curate." Perspicaciously adapting the tradition, Moore succeeds in a way of writing that is "curious" in all senses of that word: deeply religious and moral, minutely skillful, inquisitive, and one of a kind.

2 ·

Worlds of Strife:
The Poetry of Elizabeth Bishop and George Herbert

I was entangled in the world of strife,
Before I had the power to change my life.
  GEORGE HERBERT, "AFFLICTION (I)"[1]

ALMOST IN THE WAY THAT BEATRICE, clothed in "decorous and delicate crimson," appeared to the youthful Dante,[2] the figure of George Herbert, with curled hair and in red satin, appeared in a dream to the twenty-four-year-old Elizabeth Bishop: "Dreamed I had a long conversation on meter with George Herbert: we discussed the differences between his and Donne's and touched upon Miss Moore's, which was felt, in the dream, to beat Donne's but not his. This may have been subconscious politeness on my part. He had curls and was wearing a beautiful dark red satin coat. He said he would be "useful" to me. . . . Praise God."[3]

This obviously cherished dream is one of very few recorded by Bishop in her early (1934-1936) journal; and throughout her career in both published and unpublished remarks, Bishop would confirm Herbert's continuing and powerful presence in her life. A 1942 letter to Marianne Moore suggests, for example, that for Bishop George Herbert's poetry almost supplanted psychotherapy: "Did I ever show you the book I had by Dr. Karen Horney (the one I went to) called, I think, *The Neurotic Personality of Our Time*. . . . I had infinitely rather approach such things from the Christian viewpoint, myself—the trouble is I've never been able to find the books, except Herbert."[4] A 1957 letter to Robert Lowell, thanking him for the special gift of a family edition of Herbert, reveals that Bishop was in the habit of keeping *The Temple* near her the way some people keep the Bible: "I've been reading a lot in Herbert— this is the first time I'd ever gone travelling without him so it is nice to have him again."[5] And toward the end of her career, in a 1974 talk entitled "Influences" for the Academy of American Poets, Bishop remembered her early attraction to George Herbert's poetry and averred her lasting affection:

> When I was fourteen or so, I went to summer camp on Cape Cod. Every summer at this camp they made one trip. They would take us to Provincetown. There was a bookshop that had secondhand books, and I looked around and I bought a little volume of Herbert. I had never heard of him at that point, before I went away to boarding school. I read some of his things there in the bookshop and liked them so much I bought the book. . . . Herbert has always been one of my favorite poets, if not my favorite.[6]

But how could the seventeenth-century rector of Bemerton prove "useful" to the ambitious young poet, newly graduated from Vassar, who dreamed that he made her this promise? Clearly, it is more than a matter of "meter," the subject of conversation in Bishop's wonderful and strangely decorous dream.

Except for her brief remark about "subconscious politeness," Bishop left the dream uncommented upon in her journal, and we cannot know what might have been altered or suppressed in its recording. But familiarity with her life and work inevitably suggests a few interpretations. One senses here the young poet's already well-developed literary self-definition (she knows what literary company she keeps, which poets are important to her own project) and her unusual confidence (she feels that she belongs naturally in this eminent company). More particularly, Herbert's appearance in a red satin robe (a costume with ecclesiastical associations) suggests a visual pun on Bishop's surname, and so a personal identification of some sort with this long-admired religious poet. That Moore's meter "was felt, in the dream, to beat Donne's, but not Herbert's," we might then see as expressive of the young dreamer's quite natural literary competitiveness with her more established contemporary. But Bishop's characteristically tentative and characteristically humorous suggestion that Herbert's preeminent position "may have been subconscious politeness on my part" also leaves room for the possibility that, outside of the dream, she might view Moore as Herbert's (and as her own) superior. The dream record thus insists upon the notion of a literary hierarchy even as it resists establishing that hierarchy clearly.

Intertwined in the dream with this complex of literary allegiances and literary ambition are, of course, other longings. Herbert comes to Bishop as an unthreatening, charmingly androgynous figure. (How much more unlikely to imagine bold John Donne in this girlish guise than the country parson whose softer-spoken, chaste verses are full of the adjective "sweet.") The romantic but sexually defused figure is rather childlike with its curls; it is also maternal in both its feminine aspect and guiding function. And this helpful and feminized version of Herbert stands beside that other maternal figure, Bishop's newly acquired (forty-seven-year-old) friend and mentor, Marianne Moore. The dream vision then, permeated by poetic aspiration and romantic longing, would seem also to embody a retrospective yearning in this young woman whose childhood had lacked reassuring continuity and whose mother, taken from her when she was five years old, had died in a mental institution just a year before the dream.[7]

Bishop's readers consistently point to the sense of home-lessness and retrospective yearning that suffuses her poetry—David Kalstone, for instance, observing that "Bishop's precise explorations become a way of countering and en-countering a lost world."[8] Bishop is a nostalgic writer, but less sentimental and certainly much less "confessional" than other poets of her generation obsessed with recapturing or rectifying the experiences of childhood. (One might think of Randall Jarrell's *The Lost World* in this connection, or of Theodore Roethke's "The Lost Son.") Subtly expressed in assiduously impersonal description, her personal losses are persistently bound up with a sense of vanished orthodox Christian belief, with what she would call (in "The Bight") "old correspondences." And this habitual association is unsurprising when we consider that Bishop was, as she said, "full of hymns" from her earliest years in Nova Scotia, when she accompanied her grandfather to both Presbyterian and Baptist churches. Her favorite poetry—by Moore, Herbert, Donne, and also Hopkins—is de-voutly Christian. Although Bishop declared, "I'm not the slightest bit religious,"[9] the unremittingly skeptical poems of this confirmed unbeliever (see her poem "The Unbe-liever") are nevertheless full of religious allusions and stud-ded with churches or churchlike objects. For example, her self-consciously self-reflexive "Monument" stands "four-sided, stiff, ecclesiastical"; "Cape Breton" has "little white churches . . . dropped into the matted hills/like lost quartz arrowheads"; the "grand, otherworldly" female animal in "The Moose" is

> Towering, antlerless,
> high as a church,
> homely as a house
> (or, safe as houses).

The precarious, fleeting, often quietly humorous moments of grace in Bishop's poetry—such as this dreamlike encoun-ter between bus passengers and a moose on the road at night—generally counter a sense of loss by combining affectionate description of natural creatures or objects, Christian allusiveness, and maternal or homey imagery.

Herbert's poetry of spiritual struggle, replete nevertheless with what Bishop called "homely images and their solidity," clearly appealed to her conjoined religious nostalgia and longing for the lost world of home; and her own poetry shows both fairly obvious and not-so-obvious signs of her return over time to Herbert's *The Temple* as a comfort and a resource. For some more overt echoes and resemblances, there are Bishop's borrowing of occasional quotations; her adoption of a kind of Herbertian childlike persona and fantasticality; a Herbert-like use of simple diction, paradox and punning, and frequent interrogatives; a similar general obsession with inner, spiritual conflict. There are, however, other examples in Bishop's work that demonstrate genuinely different, even antithetical praxis. For one thing, although her more-or-less five- and three-beat lines may remind us of Herbert's experiments with mixed meters or hymn meters, she employs a less certain, more makeshift free verse form. She includes in her poems many nonemblematic, often teasingly "irrevelant," minute physical descriptions. And repeatedly she invokes, with her modern adaptation of metaphysical wit, an ironic sense of God's absence rather than presence. Although it is always problematic to argue from the negative, Bishop's formal and tonal choices in these instances are so self-consciously opposed to Herbert's that they suggest his presence even in his absence: that is, she is responding to her orthodox Christian model by deliberately positioning herself—to varying degrees at different moments—in opposition to him. These two kinds of adaptation (both the positive and the negative) are often so entangled in Bishop's work that they cannot be readily teased apart. The attention that Bishop paid to specific devices and strategies she found in Herbert's poetry, both by imitating and by self-consciously evading them, also suggests that her private poetic agenda was to produce an analogous, but more naturalistic and skeptical body of work—to construct for another time another kind of *Temple*.

We can see Bishop's adaptation of Herbert as early as 1936 in "The Weed," her self-avowed imitation of his "Love Unknown."[10] Bishop's poem presents a sort of amalgam of her long-standing interest in Herbert and her fascination with the then current continental surrealist movement, as these remarks from an interview some thirty years after the poem's composition indicate:

> *Miss Bishop:* Some of Herbert's poems strike me as almost surrealistic, "Love Unknown," for instance. (I was much interested in surrealism in the '30s.)
> *Interviewer:* Do you owe any of your poems to Herbert?
> *Miss Bishop:* Yes, I think so. "The Weed" is modelled somewhat on "Love Unknown." There are probably others.[11]

Both "Love Unknown" and "The Weed" are concerned with spiritual struggle and transformation, and both recount violent, dreamlike ordeals in which the passive speaker's heart has been mangled. In Herbert's poem the heart is variously "washt, and wrung," boiled and pricked; in Bishop's dream narrative it is "split apart" by a fast-growing, talking weed. Certainly among their authors' strangest, these poems depict ultimate subjection, the breaking of the individual heart or spirit. But the subjugating or destructive power (the Lord's will in Herbert's poem, some mysterious force associated with nature in Bishop's) is also constructive. Herbert's "Master" sees to it that the proffered heart is mutilated only to be made anew: it becomes acceptable by being made more susceptible to divine love ("new, tender, quick"). And the weed that severs Bishop's heart renews her spirit also—first waking her "from desperate sleep," then literally getting her creative juices flowing. Her heart, which "broke a flood of water" (suggestive of a woman "breaking water" before childbirth) becomes the source of "two rivers" that seem to gush fresh poetic material:

. . . each drop contained a light,
a small illuminated scene;
the weed-deflected stream was made
itself of racing images.

Like so many phrases in Bishop's poetry, "small illuminated scene" carries nostalgic religious associations (here we may think of some scene from an illuminated manuscript); but the transformation in "The Weed," unlike that in Herbert's poem, is not strictly speaking a religious transformation. For Bishop—whose preoccupation with water, dew and tears in such poems as "The Weed," "The Man-Moth," "At the Fishhouses," "Songs for a Colored Singer (IV)," and "Sestina" links her to the seventeenth-century Christian poetry preoccupied with eyes and tears—water may represent spiritual renewal or rebirth, a sort of baptism.[12] However, for her this "baptism," rather than bringing the promise of immortality and union with God, results in ceaseless isolated invention, weary productivity. Taking a more secular notion of "change of heart" as her subject (imaginative and artistic reawakening rather than Christian revitalization), Bishop here adopts Herbert's "almost surrealistic" approach in "Love Unknown" to the portrayal of inner reality.

She borrows, too, Herbert's mix of extraordinary incident with ordinary speech. "Love Unknown," as Bishop observes, "is fantastic, and it is simple language. It's conversation, somebody talking to somebody, and the friend speaks up from time to time."[13] Herbert's almost frenetically ingenious poem begins very simply, with a social invitation: "Deare Friend, sit down, the tale is long and sad." Imitating Herbert's polite conversational interjections and use of monosyllables, Bishop sets up the following exchange between puzzled narrator and heartrending plant at the end of "The Weed" (the sense of rueful comedy is her own):

"What are you doing there?" I asked.
It lifted its head all dripping wet

(with my own thoughts?)
and answered then: "I grow," it said,
"but to divide your heart again."

A buried couplet—"then"/"again"—inside the (inconclusive) conclusion of this occasionally rhymed and roughly tetrameter poem points to Bishop's self-conscious modification of Herbert's poetic form in "Love Unknown": alternately rhymed pentameter with a final couplet. If, in spite of its imagistic inventiveness and tone of bittersweet bravado, "The Weed" finally seems somewhat timid in its cautious adaptation of Herbert and in its refusal to establish (as Herbert's religious poem does establish) a sense of the source of the narrator's psychological upheaval, Bishop's early admiring imitation shows her assimilating certain strategies that will continue to prove useful. Like Herbert's allegorical narrative, "The Weed" plays polite surface against disruptive depth. It too deploys matter-of-fact, simple language to offer a strange and violent vision of interior life.

Bishop once again turned to "Love Unknown" when asked to select a favorite poem that she felt would be revealing of her own practices for Richard Howard and Thomas Victor's 1974 anthology, *Preferences*. For that book, however, she offered as a companion piece to Herbert's poem not "The Weed" but "In the Waiting Room," a mature piece that shows her more confident adaptation of Herbert's poetics of spiritual struggle. In his "Comment" for *Preferences*, Richard Howard calls attention to the process of "tempering" embodied in each writer's work:

> The oracle [in Bishop's "Waiting Room"] is, in part, the *National Geographic*, whose "volcano,/ black, and full of ashes;/ . . . spilling over/in rivulets of fire," just like Herbert's "font, wherein did fall/A stream of blood, which issued from the side/of a great rock," functions as an instrument of tempering. Pain, war, all the horrors of the flesh, the inadequacies of mere self-hood . . . these are the means by which we

are brought home to ourselves as we must be if we are
authentically alive, "new, tender, quick."[14]

A transforming violence is at the heart of these poets'
productions. Images of violence evoke an energy that, as
Howard suggests, "collocates, fuses" (the volcano which
introduces the young Bishop to her appalling membership
in the human community; the font, which prepares Herbert for participation in the sacraments of the Church). At
the same time, these images also express emphatic resistance to such fusion. Bishop's defiant armadillo (in her
poem "The Armadillo") with "weak mailed fist/clenched
ignorant against the sky," like Herbert's defiant priest (in
"The Collar") who "struck the board and cry'd, No
more," represents this embattled other side. Both Bishop
and Herbert write out of, and about, the ongoing war—or,
occasionally, the peace—between an individual will and
some other, extraordinarily powerful force. Out of this
essential conflict comes each poet's small but elegant and
eloquent body of work, each poet's "world of strife."[15]

The conflicting forces in these respective worlds are, of
course, unlike. Over and over, Herbert's poems attempt to
resolve the combative difference between the willful human speaker and his God, between "mine" and "thine."[16]
Bishop inherits the more secular terms of conflict in her
world from Wordsworth and other Romantic poets, who,
as René Wellek puts it, "all see the implication of imagination, symbol, myth and organic nature, and see it as part of
the great endeavor to overcome the split between subject
and object, the self and the world, the conscious and the
unconscious."[17] "The Weed," in fact, represents metaphorically a sort of ceaseless tug-of-war between these large
opposing forces. Robert Pinsky locates in Bishop's later
poems and particularly in her "In the Waiting Room," a
more specific—and more specifically *socially* anxious—
version of the Romantic endeavor when he speaks of "the
contest—or truce, or trade-agreement between the single

human soul on the one hand and the world of artifacts and other people."[18] "In the Waiting Room" dramatically portrays the disorienting experience of such a split:

> But I felt: you are an *I*,
> you are an *Elizabeth,*
> you are one of *them.*
> *Why* should you be one, too?

(One might note here Bishop's characteristically subdued and wry humor as she reinforces the notion of division with that pun on "one, two.")

Different in their expressions of individual psychologies and separate literary inheritances, the "worlds" of these two writers are nevertheless importantly alike in their persistent depiction of spiritual striving and strife, in their painstaking investigation of what one admirer of Herbert has called "inner weather."[19] Bishop's later poems are, as David Kalstone has pointed out, "more openly inner landscapes than ever before";[20] in them, the always reticent Bishop looks more frankly at her own experience, her self. "In the Waiting Room" gives us a more specific sense of the speaker's psychological anxiety than does "The Weed." It is also more formally relaxed and venturous (with its roughly three stress, free verse lines) than Bishop's early imitation, more freighted with autobiographical particulars than any Herbert poem. Once again, Bishop adapts Herbert's characteristic mix of ordinary and surreal elements to express inner conflict, but in this strategy now she is more individual and bold.

The simplicity, even flatness, of speech in this later poem is more extreme; and the situation, unlike that in Bishop's fantastic dream narrative, is insistently ordinary:

> In Worcester, Massachusetts,
> I went with Aunt Consuelo
> to keep her dentist's appointment
> and sat and waited for her
> in the dentist's waiting room.

Yet the anxious child in the dentist's office finds this quotidian setting disturbingly queer:

> —I couldn't look any higher—
> at shadowy gray knees,
> trousers and skirts and boots
> and different pairs of hands
> lying under the lamps.
> I knew that nothing stranger
> had ever happened

This is a terribly odd landscape, in which people—by a sort of violent synecdochical reduction—are seen only as agglomerations of physical parts or of objects. To this child, "pairs of hands" (which recall Eliot's "pair of ragged claws") seem as different from herself as boots or lamps; yet she knows that she herself is another of those strange agglomerations, another person "like them."

The blend of the everyday and the bizarre (or the "unlikely," to borrow Bishop's characteristically understated term) that I have been describing here as Bishop's first cautious, and then more innovative, adaptation of Herbert's practice, has been located in Bishop's oeuvre by Helen Vendler. Vendler calls attention to the characteristic "interpenetration of the domestic and the strange" in Bishop's poetry, pointing out for example that "In [her] 'Sestina,' the components are almost entirely innocent—a house, a grandmother, a child, a Little Marvel Stove, and an almanac. The strangest component, which finally renders the whole house unnatural, is tears":[21]

> But secretly, while the grandmother
> busies herself about the stove,
> the little moons fall down like tears
> from between the pages of the almanac
> into the flower bed the child
> has carefully placed in front of the house.
>
> *Time to plant tears*, says the almanac.

Bishop's introduction of tears into the grandmother's kitchen as an enigmatic, disquieting element resembles George Herbert's introduction of a shooting star into the lap of domesticity in "Artillerie":

> As I one ev'ning sat before my cell,
> Me thoughts a starre did shoot into my lap.
> I rose, and shook my clothes . . .

In Herbert's poem, of course, the star is sent by (and speaks for) God. In Bishop's sestina the "strange component" does not suggest divine intervention, but rather, as we might expect, the pathos of desperate human invention. The child and the grandmother try to fend off some unspoken grief—probably, as Vendler points out, grief over the absence of the child's parents—by making what they can: tea, conversation, a fire, pictures. And the poet seems to participate in their anxious activity by inventing multiple metaphors for the tears that they fight off and by fulfilling the requirements of an obsessive and demanding verse form.

In those poems where Herbert and Bishop take on the most frightening and enigmatic of experiences—"Death" and "First Death in Nova Scotia"—we see their most concerted attempts at domestication. Herbert's poem, psychologically tough in its acknowledgment of our human response to death as "an uncouth hideous thing," is wonderful in its transformation of death into something beautiful— even welcome as a lover ("fair and full of grace"). Speaking not as an anxious, isolated individual, but as one of the Christian community of the faithful, Herbert is able to evoke an emotionally appealing death which becomes, in a reassuringly "homely" imaginative move, a social success ("Much in request").

The domestication of death that succeeds in Herbert's poem is attempted and then made to fail in Bishop's "First Death in Nova Scotia." An imaginative child tries to see her cousin Arthur's coffin as a pleasant, sweet thing, "a little frosted cake," and to improvise comforting stories out of the objects at hand, which appeal to her sense of pattern with their red and white colors. She tells herself a story about Jack Frost painting Arthur, and she makes up a fairy tale (from the family "chromographs" of royalty) about Arthur going to some warm and gracious royal court. But death resists such cheery transformation, just as the "stuffed loon," a decoration in the family parlor, resists. The child tells herself—in a startling echo, conscious or not, of Herbert's "Much in request"—that the loon's red glass eyes are "much to be desired," and we think how a child might covet such pretty objects as collectibles, like marbles. Then she suddenly becomes aware, as she is lifted to lay a lily in her dead cousin's hand, that the loon, a sort of angel of death in this poem, is spookily "eyeing" the coffin/cake. The dressing of death that Christian faith accomplishes in Herbert's poem ("And all thy bones with beauty shall be clad") becomes here only part of a fairy tale ("their feet were well wrapped up/in the ladies' ermine trains"), and the child doesn't know whether to believe her own story or not. The poem ends not with the certainty of declarative statement as Herbert's poem does, but with a question, acknowledging the frailty of human ritualistic gestures in the face of death and the frailty of the child's own imaginative construct:

> But how could Arthur go,
> clutching his tiny lily,
> with his eyes shut up so tight
> and the roads deep in snow?

The many concrete particulars in Bishop's poem (chromographs, coffin, stuffed loon, lily) remind us of her nineteenth-century descriptive inheritance and of the more modern influences of imagism and of Marianne Moore. Her verse form (short, three-beat lines with occasional scattered rhymes) draws on modernist free verse experimentation, particularly on Williams's short lines, and is closely related to the line that her friend Robert Lowell (following Bishop's earlier example) employed in his *Life Studies*; the choice of subject—an early childhood memory, narrated in the first person—may be influenced by Lowell's autobiographical *Studies*.[22] But more like her seventeenth-century model, Bishop here displays a spiritual yearning as well as a psychological toughness; she too combines a quiet simplicity—one might almost say a "chastity"—of style with the refusal to compromise complexity.

In all her writing, Bishop adopts that "naturalness of tone" that she cited and admired in Herbert's work.[23] "Naturalness" is, of course, a problematic standard to impose on the unnatural art of written composition, but we know what Bishop means. As poet and priest, George Herbert disavows secular love poetry, substituting "plain" speech for "curled" or ornate language.[24] With his adoption of what Yvor Winters calls the "plain style," Herbert registers a moral decision, a Christian repudiation of *Vanitas*.[25] In "Love Unknown," the colloquial conversation also makes more accessible the strangeness and violence of religious transformation. In "The Collar," the immediacy and plainness of the "child's" final response ("And I re-ply'd, *My Lord*") make us feel how near at hand the ease of spiritual at-homeness can sometimes be for the believing Christian. Linking this simplicity of language (never simplicity of thought) to a "child" or childlike speaker, Herbert can present man's relation to God as a bond of filial obedience and family affection.

In a letter to Marianne Moore, Bishop expressed her admiration for Herbert's *social* bearing, his tactful manners and quiet gentility: "The negroes [in Florida] have such soft voices and such beautifully tactful manners—I suppose it is farfetched, but their attitude keeps reminding me of the *tone* of George Herbert."[26] She herself chooses "simple language," one feels, largely as a matter of personal taste— a temperamental aversion to the meretricious or garish. But her "naturalness of tone," like Herbert's, is also a matter of decorous comportment in relation to some larger power. Adjuring grandeur and floridity, Bishop is humble in the presence of an incomprehensible and indomitable world. Her contemporary version of the plain style registers her modest sense of the limits of rhetorical power, even as it expresses her pertinacious compulsion to order: through simple language, to make the world more understandable or comical or manageable.

"In the Waiting Room," for example, carries simplicity of language to its extreme in an extremely unnerving situation. Very carefully, in the most prosaic phrases, times and places are labelled: "In Worcester, Massachusetts"; "I said to myself: three days/and you'll be seven years old"; "it was still the fifth/of February, 1918." In one way, the language of this poem seems to suggest that one can make the terrifying and strange normal and orderly by putting ordinary words in ordinary places. In another way, it suggests (by its halting, anxious flatness and its flashes of menacing imagery) that just beneath the individual attempt at rational arrangement or domestication is intractable otherness, ready to erupt like the volcano pictured in the dentist's office copy of the *National Geographic*.

The child in the waiting room appears orphaned (no mother or father enters the picture, only her "foolish aunt"), and this makes her attempt to domesticate the strange particularly poignant—even more so when we remember that Elizabeth Bishop herself was brought up not by her parents but by an assortment of relations. The grave and literate child in this poem, like the oddly whimsical and studiously plainspoken adult in "Crusoe in England," is obviously an autobiographical figure. And "The War" mentioned at the end of "In the Waiting Room" evokes Bishop's embattled poetic stance, just as Crusoe's fashioning of makeshift entertainments and tools suggests her poetic fashioning. Of course, Bishop's employment of the intuitive wise child figure in such poems as "First Death in

Nova Scotia" and "In the Waiting Room" owes something to Romantic poetry, and her use of personae in general (e.g., her Crusoe, Gentleman of Shalott, or Prodigal) is informed by her reading of Pound and Eliot. But she has also learned from George Herbert, who used dramatic self-representation to link his personal spiritual and artistic struggle with the "Bittersweet" (see Herbert's poem of that title) experience of despair and hope, rebellion and repentance shared by other Christians. Bishop's solitary, anxious, inquisitive speakers express (we come to feel) a contemporary, secular view of the paradoxically "awful but cheerful" condition of humanity.

And Bishop employs paradox in ways that remind us of her favorite seventeenth-century metaphysicals. "The Weed" that breaks her heart only to build her creative spirit acts, for example, like Herbert's "Killing and quick'-ning" God ("The Flower")—or like Donne's God (Herbert, of course, having learned from the older poet) who batters to mend, breaks to make new, and throws down to raise up. Herbert says of his God that He is "All my delight, so all my smart" ("Affliction [II]"). The natural world seems imbued with a similar paradoxical power for Elizabeth Bishop, whose alter ego Crusoe wittily christens a volcano "*Mont d'Espoir or Mount Despair.*"

T. S. Eliot explained "metaphysical wit" as involving "a recognition, implicit in the expression of every experience, of other kinds of experience which are possible."[27] The poems in *The Temple,* as Hugh Kenner has suggested, are "witty" in this sense, since they characteristically hold opposing realities in poise.[28] "The Pearl," for example, discloses Herbert's deep attraction to and familiarity with worldly learning, honor, and pleasure ("the lullings and the relishes of it") even as it expresses a religious devotion that has led and is leading the poet out of "these labyrinths" and toward his God. "The Forerunners," a poem of lingering farewell to language and this life, is extraordinarily powerful precisely because it insists upon the human tension between the poet's reluctance to let go ("Lovely en-chanting language, sugar-cane,/Hony of roses, whither wilt thou flie?") and his Christian acceptance ("Go birds of spring: let winter have his fee;/ Let a bleak paleness chalk the door").

Bishop in turn offers more than one version of or vision of reality at a time by counterpointing some apparent con-tradictions. However, whereas Herbert's wit may be seen as part of his ongoing attempt to bring the human mind and heart into proper "temper" or alignment with his Christian Lord, Bishop's modern version of metaphysical wit is less hopeful. Lacking the belief that there is a divine dispensation with which her own disposition might finally harmonize, she exposes irresolvable psychological conflicts, dubieties, gaps or ironies. In her longest and most ambitious poem, "Crusoe in England," for example, she evokes the uneasy relationship between self and other, delineating this familiar conflict in complicated terms. In one way, the objective world is Crusoe's island on which he is a sort of Adam, ascribing meanings and names. In another way, the volcanic island itself (meager and sustaining, boring and interesting, resented and cherished) becomes the inner, subjective world of the "single human soul," and England, to which Crusoe returns, becomes the other world, out there. Among other things, this poem is about social and antisocial impulses—those forces of affiliation and autonomy that clashed in "In the Waiting Room." On his island, "a sort of cloud-dump" where there is just "one kind of everything," Crusoe does not feel a Wordsworthian "bliss of solitude." On the one hand, he dreams "of food/and love," and when Friday finally arrives (still "one kind," one gender), he wishes for sexual union and procreation:

> Friday was nice.
> Friday was nice, and we were friends.
> If only he had been a woman!
> I wanted to propagate my kind,
> and so did he, I think, poor boy.

On the other hand, Crusoe has dreams that suggest violent, antisocial impulses and anxiety about generation, endless reproduction:

> . . . But then I'd dream of things
> like slitting a baby's throat, mistaking it
> for a baby goat. I'd have
> nightmares of other islands
> stretching away from mine, infinities
> of islands, islands spawning islands,
> like frogs' eggs turning into polliwogs
> of islands . . .

(The passage, of course, evokes the anxieties and fatigues of artistic as well as biological generation.) Here and elsewhere in her poetry, Bishop reinforces complexity of view by using the psychoanalytically aware trick of sound association to effect a sort of dreamlike double take: "baby's throat . . . baby goat"; "*Mont d'Espoir* or *Mount Despair*"; "introspection . . . or retrospection" ("Paris, 7 A.M."); "Shadows, or are they shallows" ("The Map").

Bishop even adopts the celebrated metaphysical pun as yet another means for achieving a kind of complexity in simplicity. George Herbert suggests, for example, when he calls a poem "The Temper," the process by which his speaker moves from complaint to trust, becoming more properly conjoined with or attuned to his Lord's will because he has been "tempered" (i.e., tuned like a musical instrument, or transformed through hardship or through applications of heat and cold like steel). With the word "collar," Herbert evokes the strength of his priestly bond to God as well as his chafing rebelliousness (his fit of choler). When on her birthday Elizabeth Bishop describes a bay as littered with "old correspondences" ("The Bight"), she shows attentiveness to a bit of the world outside herself (the bay is cluttered with debris, rather like her cluttered desk);[29] she wittily and wickedly puns on Baudelaire's more breathlessly exalted symbolist "Correspondences" (Baudelaire having been referred to earlier in the poem); and she lets us know in two reticent words how freighted with loss, bitterness, humor, and religious nostalgia is her own middle age. Describing her goofy but sweetly grave encounters with a seal in "At the Fishhouses," Bishop similarly loads the word "immersion":

> He was curious about me. He was interested in music;
> like me a believer in total immersion,
> so I used to sing him Baptist hymns.
> I also sang "A Mighty Fortress Is Our God."
> He stood up in the water and regarded me
> steadily, moving his head a little.

The seal's ease in its natural element, the poet's absorption in her material, and the practice of baptism by total submersion: punning freely, one might say that these lines invite us to regard all three forms of immersion associated here with the seal as *saelig* or "silly," in all the modern and archaic Anglo-Saxon senses of that word: rather ludicrous, simple, somewhat feebleminded or foolish, happy as well as hapless—and blessed.

Although by her own description "not the slightest bit religious," Bishop was, like George Herbert who announced his dedication to religious poetry rather than courtly love poetry in the sonnets preserved in Walton's *Life*, dedicated to a poetry of *spirit* from the outset of her writing career. Here is an entry from the journal that she kept just after her 1934 graduation from college:

> It's a question of using the poet's proper material, with which he's equipped by nature, i.e., immediate, intense physical reactions, a sense of metaphor and decoration in everything—to express something not of them—something, I suppose, *spiritual*. But it proceeds from the material, the material eaten out with acid, pulled down from underneath, made to perform and always kept in order, in its place. Sometimes it cannot be made to indicate its spiritual goal clearly (some of

Hopkins', say, where the point seems to be missing) but even then the spiritual must be felt. Miss Moore does this—but occasionally I think, the super-material content in her poems is too easy for the material involved,—it could have meant more. The other way—of using the supposedly "spiritual"—the beautiful, the nostalgic, the ideal and *poetic,* to produce the *material* is the way of the Romantic, I think—and a great perversity. This may be capable of being treated by a mere studying of similes and metaphor—This is why genuine religious poetry seems to be about as far as poetry can go—and as good as it can be—it also explains the dangers of love poetry.[30]

In this densely packed passage, the ambitious young poet is pulling together a wide variety of literary influences to shape a personal poetics. She imagines an ideal poetry, the sort she herself wishes to write. It would begin with carefully considered and controlled material and proceed toward some clear but not "too easy" spiritual goal. (This method, which combines observation with meditation, is closely related to the practices of Saint Ignatius Loyola, on whose *Spiritual Exercises* the young poet took careful notes.)[31] With critical incisiveness and sternness surprising in one so young and so publicly deferential, Bishop assesses two poets who, in their separate, idiosyncratic ways, approximate her ideal: Hopkins (a less enduring early influence than Herbert) and her new mentor, Marianne Moore. The self-consciously "scientific" description of properly manipulated material in this journal entry recalls William Carlos Williams's 1925 praise of Moore's brand of modernism, with which Bishop was surely familiar: "With Miss Moore a word is a word most when it is separated out by science, treated with acid to remove the smudges, washed, dried, and placed right side up on a clean surface."[32] Bishop reaffirms Dr. Williams's praise, even as she expresses some reservation about Moore's management of "super-material" content. She then condemns "the Romantic" approach, implicating all muzzily "poetic" writing, including any facile nineteenth-century Romantic poetizing. Clearly, the young woman who composed this journal entry felt allegiance to a modernist aesthetic of particularity and precision as well as to the "genuine religious poetry" of the seventeenth century.

And indeed Bishop seems to acknowledge her difference from as well as her debt to her favorite seventeenth-century religious poet with the very first poem in her first book. "The Map" (in *North & South* and then again as the first poem in the 1969 edition of *The Complete Poems*) is a sort of twentieth-century counterpart of the first poem in *The Church*, that collection of religious lyrics that constitutes the body of Herbert's *The Temple*. Each poem launches a writing project by describing that project with a single metaphor—a metaphor expressive of the author's deepest convictions about the relation of artistic activity to spiritual life.

Whatever else one might say about "The Altar," which Richard Strier has called "one of Herbert's most puzzling poems,"[33] it is clearly concerned with the relation between (mere) human invention and the creative and transformative power of God.[34] "The Altar," like the altar in a church, is a locus for praise, prayer, and communion. By placing this poem at the beginning of his collection—as the first thing seen when entering his Church—Herbert expresses his conviction that human artistic endeavor is properly a means for religious reflection and rededication, an expression of yearning along the vertical axis from man to God, from "mine" to "thine."

Of course Bishop's "The Map" is not spiritual in the sense that Herbert's "The Altar" is spiritual: there is nothing specifically religious about either its form or its content. It is not even, like so many of Bishop's poems, openly nostalgic about religion (although "The Imaginary Iceberg"—immediately following "The Map" in both *North & South* and *The Complete Poems*—may, with its concluding metaphor about "the soul," retroactively color our interpretation). Precisely because of its insistently secular character, this early poem provides us with a clear sense of Bishop's adaptation of, and variation on, her favorite religious poetry. Although relatively slight in view of her later, richer work, "The Map" thus serves an important introductory function.

By launching her own collection(s) of poetry with "The Map," Bishop indicates through metaphor that her work will be obsessed with the question of location, a question that Herbert's *The Temple* (with its "Church-Porch" and then its "Altar") resolves at the outset. Bishop's poem introduces her reader to a text or "world" in which the human spirit attempts to locate itself or to find "home," not in relation to a single vertical axis (Herbert's "silk twist" from God to Man), but rather in relation to the horizontal axes defined by the four cardinal directions on a cartographer's schematic representation. Obviously, a map—with its morally arbitrary directions, or rather with its lack of moral direction—is baffling as a spiritual "homing" device. "Topography," as Bishop writes here, "displays no favorites: North's as near as West." Without Herbert's orthodox religious orientation, Bishop's metaphorical counterpart to "The Altar" suggests, we are quite literally left to our own devices—devices more than likely to leave us, as the repeated interrogatives in this poem adumbrate, with a sense of bewilderment and wilderment, of restless questioning and quest.

Nevertheless, Bishop's admiration for and emulation of the artifact that she so absorbedly describes in her poem is obvious. With "The Map," Bishop tells us that she subscribes to modernist values of particularity and precision: like mapmaking, her poetry aims at scrupulous re-presentation of the physical world. We find here a self-effacing attentiveness to objective reality (akin to the mapmaker's accuracies); we find also the assertion of an imagination that quietly, but persistently, refashions that reality in its own subjective—and frequently domestic—terms (terms such as "emotion" or "yard-goods"). This complex interplay between imagination and object, between mind and world, is much like the complex interdependence between land and sea that Bishop quizzically projects upon the cartographer's representation:

> Land lies in water; it is shadowed green.
> Shadows, or are they shallows, at its edges
> showing the line of long sea-weeded ledges
> where weeds hang to the simple blue from green.
> Or does the land lean down to lift the sea from under,
> drawing it unperturbed around itself?
> Along the fine tan sandy shelf
> is the land tugging at the sea from under?

Does the sea support the land, or does the land support the sea? Does reality determine our perceptions, or do our perceptions determine reality? Bishop's poem raises these questions, which it must decline to answer.

"The Map" may begin in meticulous, impersonal description, but, as Sybil P. Estess points out, "the meaning of 'The Map' extends far beyond a mere realistic description of the literal object. This poem delineates the nature of a relationship between objective reality and one's subjective and imaginative assimilation of such 'facts.' "[35] Keeping in mind the salient terms from Bishop's early journal entry, we might say that "The Map" shows both its author's careful consideration of "material" and her attention to desires and dilemmas that are inward and "spiritual."

Bishop's "The Map," then, introduces a poetry of spirit—of psychological reflection, metaphysical and moral inquiry—which self-consciously departs from Herbert's orthodox Christian poetry. If Herbert's "The Altar" focusses on the disjunction or correspondence between human and divine fashioning, Bishop's twentieth-century counterpart focusses solely on human construction—on what we may compose out of the complex interplay of mind and world. If Herbert shows us what it means to praise God appropriately or decorously, Bishop demonstrates the appropriate action of an individual soul or spirit in a desacralized world. Paying meticulous attention to the physical particulars of that world while making imaginative sense (and imaginative play) out of what she sees, Bishop shows us a way of respecting objective reality without giving way—or giving sway—to mere thingness. To be "observant" in this sense (attentive at once to geographical features and to that other landscape, inside) is almost a form of religious observance.

Almost. Bishop's is a world of partial satisfactions, incompleted quests. "Arrival at Santos," the first poem in *Questions of Travel*, inconclusively concludes with an immediate departure: "We leave Santos at once;/we are driving to the interior." As David Kalstone has pointed out, "interior" is a pun, implying both geographical and psychological penetration.[36] But any final destination or final understanding remains as unattainable as Bishop's "proto-dream-house" in "The End of March." (The punning title of this poem from *Geography III* designates a time of year and also suggests, ironically, the goal or termination of all travel, or travail.) Bishop says of her dream-house, a shack on the beach, which she nevertheless envisions as an ideal mental and physical resting place, "Many things about this place are dubious." "The End of March"—so much about pairs of things and the number two (e.g., a walk out and a walk back; "two bare rooms"; "blue flame . . . doubled in the window")—reactivates the etymological connection between "dubious" and "duo."[37] It makes us see "home" as an imaginative construct composed of double and conflicted desires: the wish to be part of things and the yearning to be apart from them; the urge to create and the need to rest. Her dilapidated "crypto-dream-house"—which calls up every child's sometime fantasy of cheerful self-sufficiency—is an extraordinarily modest version of Heaven, an unassuming shadow of Herbert's "hive of sweetness" (see Herbert's "Home"). Yet for her even this ragtag dream proves "impossible":

> And that day the wind was much too cold
> even to get that far,
> and of course the house was boarded up.

Turning, having to walk back in March wind, Bishop observes a momentary natural phenomenon, a sort of rainbow (decidedly too ordinary and unobtrusive to be called a "sign"):

> For just a minute, set in their bezels of sand,
> the drab, damp, scattered stones
> were multi-colored

Then, as if to demonstrate a moral option that remains available even in the midst of loss, her imagination recommences its serious, as well as playful, occupation of making do by making up another fiction, about "the lion sun":

> —a sun who'd walked the beach the last low tide,
> making those big, majestic paw-prints,
> who perhaps had batted a kite out of the sky to play with.

By carefully qualifying her conceits or invented correspondences with words such as *seems, if,* and *perhaps,* Bishop consistently suggests that meanings may be posited (indeed, since we need them, they *must* be), but they may not be positively or permanently asserted.

What remain permanently are questions, as her early poem, "The Map," suggested. Bishop's anxious child in "In the Waiting Room" is full of questions—not unlike Herbert's protesting priest in "The Collar" ("What? shall I ever sigh and pine?" "Shall I be still in suit?")—but her questions remain unanswered and unanswerable:[38]

> Why should I be my aunt,
> or me, or anyone?
> What similarities—
> boots, hands, the family voice
> I felt in my throat, or even
> the *National Geographic*
> and those awful hanging breasts—

> held us all together
> or made us all just one?
> . . . .
> How had I come to be here,
> like them, and overhear
> a cry of pain that could have
> got loud and worse but hadn't?

These appear in Bishop's final book, which opens with a long list of questions from an 1884 geography textbook—

> In what direction is the Volcano? The Cape? The Bay? The Lake? The Strait? The Mountains? The Isthmus?
> What is in the East? In the West? In the South? In the North?
> In the Northwest? In the Southeast? In the Northeast? In the Southwest?

—and which closes still obsessed by the interrogative mode. In "Five Flights Up," Bishop notes with mixed amusement and jealousy two unconscious, and untrammeled, creatures—a "little black dog" and an "unknown bird":

>   . . . the bird inquires
> once or twice, quavering.
> Questions—if that is what they are—
> answered directly, simply,
> by day itself.

In Herbert's "world of strife," human questioning and questing can have an end: the struggle with a God who deals out affliction and death (a struggle that we find dramatically embodied in so many of Herbert's poems) finds resolution in traditional, if difficult, Christian faith. For Elizabeth Bishop, the struggle for definition and belonging and order has no evident resolution beyond the provisional human constructs of art—constructs like her "Monument" or "Map," rather than Herbert's "Altar." Bishop's "world"—from early poems such as "The Gentleman of Shalott" or "Chemin de Fer" to later, more complex and moving ones such as "One Art" or "The End of March"—is haunted by a sense of separation, division, halfness; yet it attests to repeated efforts, which often seem quite brave, not to succumb to the dulled heart and mind of mere stoic pessimism. A longing for wholeness and at-homeness so impels Elizabeth Bishop's poetry that all of her anxious, attentive "Questions of Travel" (collectively, a twentieth-century account of the "heart in pilgrimage") come to seem analogous to George Herbert's more ortho-dox Christian poetry, which we might refer to collectively (borrowing the title of the poem in which Herbert alludes to "the heart in pilgrimage") as his "Prayer."

3 .

Re-seeing the Sea:
Marianne Moore's "A Grave"
as a Re-vision of the Tradition

"MAN LOOKING INTO THE SEA" begins Marianne Moore's first published version of "A Grave" ("A Graveyard," *The Dial*, July 1921). This version as well as another, earlier version, which was resurrected and printed by Ezra Pound in Milan in 1932, are both in turn revisions of Moore's unpublished "A Graveyard in the Middle of the Sea," produced between September 1916 and September 1918. The *Dial* poem itself was slightly revised before appearing in final form in her 1924 book, *Observations*.[1] All versions are obsessed with looking and the return of a look, with seeing and seeing again. The pun on *sea* itself, activated in the opening phrase—"Man looking into the sea"—is one compressed example of the way we are ourselves made to re-view words and concepts as we read this poem. "A Grave," then, with its preoccupation with viewing and re-viewing and its challenging opening address to "Man," has seemed to me a compelling example of a modern woman writer's re-vision.[2] Moore here is not only a meticulous observer of the natural seascape, but also a critical observer of and wily respondent to the male-dominated poetic tradition, Romantic and post–Romantic as well.

I agree, then, with Bonnie Costello, Alicia Ostriker, and others that Moore's poetry, traditionally "feminine" in many of its strategies, is far more cannily subversive of inherited values than either early, and predominantly male, criticism or most of the more recent feminist criticism has acknowledged.[3] Male critics have tended to write of Moore in a manner displaying affection, even genuine admiration, tinged with condescension. One thinks, for example, of T. S. Eliot's 1923 pronouncement: "And there is one final, 'magnificent' compliment: Miss Moore's poetry is as 'feminine' as Christina Rossetti's, one never forgets that it is written by a woman; *but* with both one never thinks of this as anything but a positive virtue" (my emphasis).[4] (One enjoys imagining Eliot's response to a similarly telling "but" in a high-handed sentence comparing his poetry, for instance, to Donne's—both there judged as markedly, but surprisingly tolerably, "masculine.") Then there are (as just a small selection) Gorham Munson's Marianne Moore, a "minor poet" of "idiosyncratic behavior";[5] John Unterecker's "mistress of quirks and oddities";[6] and Roy Harvey Pearce's "lady-like" poet, possessed of a "fussy modesty."[7] We can probably identify what these critics are responding to in Moore's work, but their tone is paternalistically dismissive. Their Marianne Moore seems a bizarre, oxymoronic figure, somehow significantly trivial—a sort of Munchkin Queen of poetry. They seem to be discussing a body of work that they do not, at bottom, take seriously.

Turning to feminist critics for an alternative view, until quite recently one encountered another sort of dismissiveness: the "limited" and "spinsterly" Marianne Moore of Suzanne Juhasz's criticism,[8] the "maidenly" and "discreet" Moore of Adrienne Rich's.[9] There is understandable urgency behind these dissatisfactions: those who are looking for a model of unabashed autobiographical revelation, for a call to political action, or for unambiguous passion and anger will not find them in this poet's work. But Marianne Moore has (as one might expect of such a resolutely individual and productive writer) another, bolder side. Beneath surface polish and politesse, she is also radical and revisionary. In "A Grave" both the reactionary and the revolutionary are at work—and returning to the history of this early modernist poem, attentive to the poet's persistently double nature, it is possible to retrieve some of what Alicia Ostriker has called Moore's "challenge to traditional authority and the beauty of [her] alternative vision."[10]

Imagine a well-educated American woman sitting down early in this century to write a poem about the sea. Naturally, she is not unaware of a European tradition of poetry on this subject stretching back to Homer; naturally, she wishes to make her own contribution, to write a poem distinguished from those that have come before. She sits down and puts pen to paper—or rather, as Hugh Kenner reminds us, fingers to keys[11]—and composes the following six-line stanza:

> The cypresses of experience dead, yet indestructible by
>   circumstance; shivering and stony in
>   the water; not green
>   But white, surrounding all that is loathsome: inanimate
> Scavengers guarding permanent garbage: watched over by
>   sharks which cruise between
>   Them—petrine like death yet not so petrine as
>   patient; everything everywhere
>   Yet nothing, because nowhere; infinity defined at
>   last, still infinity because there
>   Where nothing is.

Now imagine a student facing this turbid, rather archly fatigued, extended sentence fragment on her M. A. comprehensive exam: what is going on in this passage, and to whom would you attribute it? The unlucky student would,

I think, be hard put to say. She might associate the hypo-taxis, terms of negation, and strange stanzaic shape with Moore. The lines, she might notice, assertively too long for a standard page, are tucked as often happens with Moore's poems. Given only this stanza—one of four in the earliest extant draft—she could only guess that it is, in fact, oddly shaped because characteristically syllabic (the un-likely count per line being 32, 14, 19, 19, 23, and 4). The verse does display Moore's enduringly nervous relation to rhyme (two true rhymes, an unrhymed second line, and a sibilant last line which, unknown to the student, is deli-cately echoed by a final, hissing half-rhyme in each subse-quent stanza). But (and here a wrench is thrown into our hypothetical student's Moore-works) the poet has pre-served the traditional capitalization at line beginnings. And for more serious disqualifications, what an uncharacteristic collocation of abstractions, what un-Mooreish stasis and morbidity. Here we leave the bemused student at her desk and return to Marianne Moore at hers.

Confronted with her self-assigned task, Moore has writ-ten lines peculiarly enervated and enervating. They sug-gest not only immobility in the marine setting, but also a poet nearly immobilized by inherited notions. The writer's mind, one might almost say, is a Sargasso Sea. We would be exaggerating to exclaim (as Pound does in his "Portrait d'Une Femme") that "there is nothing! In the whole and all,/Nothing that's quite your own"; but rather than con-sciously deploying reference and quotation as in so many of her poems, Moore here seems quite uncharacteristically freighted with received ideas.

Laurence Stapleton observes that this first version of "A Grave," entitled "A Graveyard in the Middle of the Sea," is "clearly indebted to Poe's 'City in the Sea.' "[12] That poem, famous (or infamous) for the line "the viol, the violet, and the vine," overindulges in morbidity the way some people overindulge in chocolate:

Lo! Death has reared himself a throne
In a strange city lying alone
Far down within the dim West,
Where the good and the bad and the worst and the best
Have gone to their eternal rest.
There shrines and palaces and towers
(Time-eaten towers that tremble not!)
Resemble nothing that is ours.
. . . .
There open fanes and gaping graves
Yawn level with the luminous waves[13]

This verse clearly resembles little that is Moore's. Yet we do
hear in her stanza uncharacteristically heavy alliteration
("guarding permanent garbage," "not so petrine as patient"); we register some variety of atmospheric morose-
ness. These are, I think, as she sits down to write, part of the
tug backwards, part of her cargo. So are Matthew Arnold
and his most famous sea poem. Writing out of the First
World War in which her Presbyterian minister brother
served as a chaplain in the navy, Moore might well recall
Arnold's "ignorant armies" and his mournful response to a
withdrawing "Sea of Faith." Here she labors under the self-
conscious burden of an Arnoldian "serious subject" and
cultural critique, taking pains to portray a sea full of "loath-
some" refuse and amoral scavengers. In yet another poem
obsessed with decay—moral and physical—and with the
sea, a contemporary of Moore's envisions his persona as a
scavenger, "a pair of ragged claws/Scuttling across the
floors of silent seas." Composed after the first appearance of
"The Love Song of J. Alfred Prufrock" in Poetry in 1915,
Moore's lines convey a similar sense of physical revulsion
and even exhibit verbal "visions and revisions" in the form
of an Eliotic stutter ("petrine"/"petrine," "infinity"/"infinity," "nothing"/"nothing").

My point here is not that Marianne Moore was slavishly
imitating these particular poets nor, of course, that literary
influences are necessarily debilitating, but that in this first

stanza an agglomeration of post-Romantic male voices is entrammeling rather than enabling. Moore, however, jettisoned the freight and began again with what had been originally her second stanza:

> Man looking into the sea, taking the view from those
>   who have as much
> right to it as you have to it yourself, it is human na-
> ture to stand in the middle of a thing . . .

She then sent the new syllabic version called "The Graveyard" (which I am assuming is essentially the same as the poem resurrected and printed in Milan in 1932) to Ezra Pound, the man who stood in the middle of the modernist movement in poetry.

Pound's answer of December 16, 1918, and Moore's prompt reply are chiefly interesting for their implications about these writers' relations to literary authority. Pound, of course, simply assumes it. Moore displays some of that female anxiety about it that Sandra Gilbert and Susan Gubar have discussed[14]—but she also displays remarkable independence and self-assurance. Obviously impressed and fascinated by her work, Pound compliments Moore ("your stuff holds my eye") and expresses thankfulness (or an unconscious competitive wish) for her eschewal of poetic volubility: "Thank God, I think you can be trusted not to pour out a flood (in the manner of dear Amy and poor old Masters)."[15] Moore responds reassuringly, with a statement that—to borrow her own characteristic double negative— we might now see as not altogether unfalse: "I grow less and less desirous of being published, produce less and have a strong feeling for letting alone what little I produce."[16] Pound authoritatively suggests the omission of conventional capitalization, and Moore, seeing his point ("To capitalize the first word of every line, is rather slavish"), substitutes small letters. But when, finding her syllabic measure attractive, Pound appropriatively inquires "whether my beginnings had anything to do with yr. metric," Moore

refuses the role of favorite female student: "The resemblance of my progress to your beginnings is an accident so
far as I can see." And when he proposes inverting the order
of the last words in her poem from "neither with volition
nor consciousness" to "neither with consciousness nor volition," she politely replies, "I am willing to make the change,
though I prefer the original order"—but privately sticks to
her guns, maintaining original order in both the *Dial* revision and later in *Observations*. Moore's use of the nouns
"volition" and "consciousness" and her decision about their
arrangement suggest, as I hope to show, a great deal about
her re-vision of the sea as an image and of Romanticism as a
literary influence.

In *Women Writers and Poetic Identity*, Margaret Homans
has delineated the special problematics of the Romantic
literary inheritance for women readers and writers:

> In Romantic poetry the self and the imagination are primary.
> During and after the Romantic period it was difficult for
> women who aspired to become poets to share in this tradition,
> not for constitutional reasons but for reasons that women
> readers found within the literature itself. Where the masculine
> self dominates and internalizes otherness, that other is fre-
> quently defined as feminine, whether she is nature, the repre-
> sentation of a human woman, or some phantom of desire. To
> be for so long the other and the object made it difficult for
> nineteenth-century women [and, as Homans also suggests,
> for twentieth-century women as well] to have their own
> subjectivity.[17]

According to Homans's formulation, woman is the silent
"other" of male-dominated Romantic poetry. Subject to
male author-ity, she becomes dissociated from her own subjectivity. (One might think here of the silent object of ado-
ration in Byron's "She walks in Beauty, like the night"; of
Shelley's garden-identified Lady in "The Sensitive Plant,"
or of Emily, his utterly idealized and internalized "heart's
sister" in "Epipsychidion"; or of Wordsworth's naturalized
Lucy.) As Rodolfo says of Mimi (who loves him for it), and

as William "oft" suggests in another genre and language about his adored and adoring sister Dorothy, "Son un poeta, ma essa poesia." Mimi lies still and pale, quietly dying of consumption while Rodolfo sings the famous final bars of *La Bohème*. Dorothy Wordsworth's beautiful and self-effacing private journals will always and understandably be dusted off and checked out of the library by the occasional reader, while her brother's poems circulate in multiple editions. Well-versed in the verses of singing men who seem to love her best when she is silent (or unpublished), or dead, how does the aspiring female writer come to terms with her inheritance? How does she distinguish herself from beautiful but mute nature and so avoid the fate of Lucy, memorialized in William Wordsworth's simultaneously consoling and terrifying elegy?

> No motion has she now, no force;
>   She neither hears nor sees;
> Rolled round in earth's diurnal course,
>   With rocks, and stones, and trees.[18]

In the final version of "A Grave," Marianne Moore adapts the terms—the dominant figures or tropes—of her Romantic inheritance in order to come to terms with it, quite literally "coming to terms" by arriving at her own powerful poetic language.[19] Keeping in mind the admittedly simplified but nevertheless useful description of Romanticism that I have plucked from Homans' text, we can see Moore's completed poem as both a continuation of that tradition and a devastating commentary upon it. Wordsworth emphasizes the dead Lucy's lack of volition ("No motion has she now, no force") and of consciousness ("She neither hears nor sees"). This double deficiency is, as Homans suggests, the horrible but ideal female state in Romantic poetry.[20] Within this particular poetic world, a powerful female acting under her own volition, such as Keats's Belle Dame or Coleridge's serpentine Geraldine, appears as a treacherous phantom: she "effeminizes" men by seducing them into unconsciousness and tractability. What Moore does is to adopt the Romantic poet's obsession with consciousness and unconsciousness, wilfulness and will-lessness, only to redistribute these traits unconventionally among man, woman, nature, and poet—and the specific strategy of her poem is radical ambiguity.

Consider, for example, the intricacy of Moore's design on the initial monosyllable:

> Man looking into the sea,
> taking the view from those who have as much right to it as
>   you have to it yourself,
> it is human nature to stand in the middle of a thing

The word *Man* here refers in part to a particular man on a particular day, as Moore's own commentary on this poem makes clear: "As for 'A Grave,' it has a significance apart from the literal origin, which was a man who placed himself between my mother and me, and the surf we were watching from the middle ledge of rocks on Monhegan Island after the storm. ('Don't be annoyed,' my mother said. 'It is human nature to stand in the middle of a thing.')"[21]

Man also contributes to our sense of "a significance apart from the literal origin" by standing for mankind or humankind—a meaning that Mrs. Moore's quoted remark about "human nature" bolsters. But *Man* of course also denotes gender, the opposite of woman—and this third sense is reinforced by the sexual suggestion of "stand in the middle of a thing," by our knowledge of the occurrence prompting the poem (a man blocking the view of two women), and by our awareness of the poem's complex history of revision. In the two extant early drafts, the noun "people" appears mid-poem:

> . . . people now at their best, whose clothes are a
> Testimony to the fact, row across them [across the bodies
>   of dead people], the blades of the oars moving to-
>   Gether like the feet of water spiders as if there
>   were no such thing as death:

But in the *Dial* revision and the final version, the operative term has changed:

> *men* lower nets, unconscious of the fact that they are
>   desecrating a grave,
> and row quickly away—the blades of the oars
> moving together like the feet of water spiders as if there
>   were no such thing as death.
>
> [my emphasis]

The action of the completed poem, then, takes us from "Man," who annoyingly asserts his volition, to "men" who act obliviously or unconsciously, and finally to the bodies of the drowned, whom we are encouraged by Moore's deployment of nouns to see as drowned *men*, possessed of neither "volition nor consciousness." Moore thus reverses a convention of Romantic poetry by relegating Man (who becomes merely one of the "dropped things" in her ocean) to the characteristically feminine role of objectified and disempowered "other." If her artfully ambiguous poem may be read as a modernist *memento mori* addressed to humankind, it may also be read as a woman writer's canny rejoinder to the male-dominated tradition—her revision of the male poet's gendered agenda. Moore's stately and mysterious sea has a strong retributive undertow.

Moore effects her revisionary reversal further by exploiting another Romantic trope, the Belle Dame sans Merci. In Keats's ballad of that name the knight, having been seduced by a mysterious lady, wakes from a ghastly dream drained of vitality "On the cold hill's side." The strange lady with "wild wild eyes" whom the knight has met "in the meads" is—like the powerfully perverse Geraldine "with serpent's eye" who springs from an old oak tree in Coleridge's "Christabel," or like the "Night-mare Life-in-Death" in his "Rime of the Ancient Mariner"—a phantom woman associated with destructive rather than nurturing nature. As figures of unchecked female volition, Keats's Belle Dame and her Coleridgean counterparts are wily,

ghostly, weirdly beautiful, and treacherous. In "A Grave,"
Moore encourages us to see the sea as another such fatal
femme.[22] Possessed of a similarly sinister ocular intensity,
the sea is "quick to return a rapacious look"—and the lines
immediately following this phrase extend the obsession
with looking (or looks), and with the particular rapaciousness of the sea:

> There are others besides you who have worn that look—
> whose expression is no longer a protest; the fish no longer
>   investigate them
> for their bones have not lasted

Endowed with a similarly ensnaring allure, the ocean is
"beautiful under networks of foam."

But while the Romantic poet's Belle Dame sans Merci
is always nefarious and inimical, Moore's re-figuring of
this figure remains equivocal. Her ocean/grave represents
death, humanity's common enemy, and yet her sea as re-
former of inherited poetic patterns acts too as nature's and
woman's ally. The heavy sibilance throughout Moore's
poem (in all versions) reminds us of the actual foaming
ocean that advances and retreats over the shingle, of the
serpentine and treacherous ladies of Romantic poetry, perhaps also of Satan, and of mortality which menaces and
circumscribes our lives. But with her continuing sound
play—"you cannot stand in the middle of this"; "repres-
sion . . . is not the most obvious characteristic of the
sea"; "their bones have not lasted"—Moore also hisses
back at man, probably at the arrogant male poet in particular, who arrogates to himself dominion, who is always
trying "to stand in the middle of a thing." By choosing,
against Pound's advice, to conclude her poem with the
word "consciousness," Moore reserves that climactic position for the quality of attentiveness to self and to "other"
that is her highest aesthetic and moral value, while giving
her sea (as retributive force) the last word, the last hiss.[23]
How like Ezra Pound, that brilliant celebrant of male will,

not to have appreciated her original word order (although the early stanzaic version that he received underlines its structural importance); how like him to have proposed that she conclude instead with "volition."[24]

If Moore exploits the traditional association of woman and nature, she also calls that time-honored trope—together with other literary complacencies—into question. Her sea, whose "wrinkles progress among themselves in a phalanx—beautiful under networks of foam," partakes of masculine militarism as well as feminine seduction. With these quick contradictory comparisons, Moore unsettles our assumptions about the nature of nature, while she deviously turns the Romantic poet's favorite tool against him. Asserting his imagination through metaphor, the Romantic poet (ranging over mountains, lakes, antique lands) in a sense colonizes the world—appropriating "otherness" and subduing it to his own purposes. By metaphorically equipping her ocean (as armed Roman legion, as negligéed temptress) and pitting it against man, Moore turns the tables on the presumptuous male writer—subjecting him to his own "subject," and so subtly mocking his delusion of dominion, of imaginative sway.

In her own use of metaphor, Moore eschews poetic imperialism. At times, as we have just seen, she employs metaphor to expose the pathetic fallaciousness of the Romantic poet's pretension. At other times, she offers an alternative form of analogizing:

> The firs stand in procession, each with an emerald turkey-
> foot at the top,
> . . . .
> the birds swim through the air at top speed, emitting
> catcalls as heretofore—

In these lines, as elsewhere throughout her work, Moore juxtaposes rather conventional anthropomorphic associations (firs in procession, birds emitting catcalls) with associations of a different order. With her startling, stacked-up comparisons of natural creatures or objects only to other natural creatures or objects (firs/emeralds/turkey feet; birds/fish/cats), Moore lets the fresh air of irrepressible "otherness" into her poem—evoking what Bonnie Costello has termed "the splendid independence of nature from our conceptual purposes."[25] Almost hallucinatory in their specificity, her fir trees (like some new brand of Christmas tree with emerald turkey-foot stars) stand in strange self-sufficiency—emblems of nature crowned only by nature.

Moore shares with the Romantic poet a passion for natural description, but her own descriptive procedures upset inherited notions about the relation of the poet to nature—making us suddenly question which is the collector (she calls the sea "a collector") and which is the collected, which is central and which peripheral. Part of her procedure is to dispose of conventional (poet-centered) notions about *dispositio,* about arrangement. The eccentric image of fir trees, for example, comes directly after the first appearance of the word *grave,* and darts peculiarly away from the gravity of the meditative situation. After the second appearance of *grave,* halfway through the poem, we come across oared boats, figured as water spiders, that "row quickly away"; and then, immediately following the single mention of "death," we meet with Moore's elaborately metaphoric "wrinkles" or waves. Collectively, these quick turns from frightening mass to fanciful minutiae—and from depth back to surface—may be seen as evidence of Moore's psychological skittishness, of that impulse in her to "row quickly away" from a disturbing and submerged subject that we sense in other poems such as "Marriage" or "The Fish."[26] And yet these imagistic dartings or digressions also signal Moore's extreme self-consciousness about poetic egocentricity. They show how the world resists any neat poetic plan, including her own plan to portray the sea metaphorically as "a well excavated grave"; and they show Moore once again (to borrow Costello's phrase) "resisting the mind's impulse to circumscribe experience."[27]

Although Moore cannot entirely resist that impulse (since every poem in some way draws its circle around a bit of experience), it is crucial to her project that she acknowledge the world's independence from the human compulsion to order—from poems, for instance, or from prayers:

> Let who will pray for fair weather to bring him home
> Aristagoras who is buried here. The sea is the sea.[28]

These lines, which Moore copied in her notebook from *The Greek Anthology* long before she began work on "A Grave," remind us of that ocean that exists apart from, not merely peripheral to, human concerns. The poet cannot stand in the middle of it or circumscribe it (write his—or her—way around it): "The sea is the sea."

This much revised early poem of Moore's feels different from later ambitious poems (e.g., "Marriage," "An Octopus," "The Jerboa," "The Pangolin"), in part because it feels more traditional: in its medium length, in the stateliness of its rhythm and the comparative ease of its syntactic unfolding; in the relative steadiness of its meditative gaze. It lacks the condensed satiric bite of early short pieces such as "To a Steam Roller" and "Pedantic Literalist," the capaciousness and more radical experimentalism of a verbal collage like "Marriage." But it does convey, in spite of its elaborate ambiguities, an immediate sense of emotional force and rhetorical cohesion, of-a-pieceness—which may be why Elizabeth Bishop (who found her own ways to extend as well as subvert the Romantic tradition) chose this poem to read as part of her 1977 talk on influences for the Academy of American Poets.[29]

"A Grave" offered Bishop, as it offers other readers, an example of how a woman well versed in the literary tradition, rather than capitulating to the convention of female silence, can wield that tradition and write her own eloquent lines. Adapting the Romantic poet's own tactics and tropes, Moore found a way to chasten his imaginative

egocentricity, replacing his "I-ness" with her less appropria-
tive, minutely observant eye. And she did this even as she
extended early modernist imagism with moral and meditative substance. The history of her work on this pivotal
poem shows her to be both a re-actionary writer (reactivat-
ing inherited literary configurations) and a re-volutionary
one (turning and twisting the male-dominated tradition,
just as her ocean causes "dropped things" to "turn and
twist"). A grave is a place where dead things are put to
rest, but this "Grave" is a locus of Moore's challenging and
active re-vision.

4 ·

Romantic Persistences and Resistances:
Elizabeth Bishop as "minor female Wordsworth"

I HAVE TRIED TO SHOW HOW, in her extended work on "A Grave," Marianne Moore turned the Romantic tradition to her own purposes by rearranging inherited power configurations and by re-figuring conventional figures or tropes. Her early poem reveals Moore's adversarial response to nineteenth-century Romanticism more clearly and completely than most, but throughout her work we find her making use of the same revisionary tactics. These tactics, I believe, bespeak Moore's humility—her acknowledgment of indebted relatedness to the very tradition with which she covertly quarrels, as well as her respect for the independence and indomitability of the natural world. A polite and paradoxically conservative radicalism characterizes the poetry of this first-generation modernist, whom Elizabeth Bishop described as possessed of a "delicately pugnacious-looking jaw."[1]

Elizabeth Bishop's poetry—more drifting, lyric, and iambic than her older friend's—is even less overtly revisionary than Marianne Moore's. But if in the work of this second-generation modernist we observe a closer kinship with certain nineteenth-century poetic practices, we also find a continuation of Moore's project of overturning conventional hierarchies and upsetting inherited notions about the relation of man to woman, woman to nature, and poet to world. Both Bishop's persistence in and resistance to Romanticism come into focus when we examine her relation to her most important precursor in that tradition, William Wordsworth.

Writing to Robert Lowell in July of 1951, Bishop links herself to her Romantic forebear in a phrase that teases us with its wry complexity:

> Your proposed trip [to Europe, beginning with a long stay in Florence] has me very ugly and envious. However, if the N Yorker takes my article—they're interested—and I earn all I hope to, there's a chance I may still get abroad in the fall—after finding a place to live here, and paying my respects to Bryn Mawr—all that's expected of me, I gather. My book is about 85% at Houghton Mifflin but I must confess it doesn't jell at all yet—maybe the other 15% will prove to be pure pectin. I am going to call it—so far—& I hope you'll approve—"Cocordance" ["Concordance"]—starting off with a poem called "Over 2,00 [2,000] Illustrations & a Complete Concordance." On reading over what I've got on hand I find *I'm really a minor female Wordsworth*—at least, I don't know anyone else who seems to be such a Nature Lover. The N Yorker I'm delighted to say, is quibbling with me over an indelicacy in a poem.[2]
>
> [my emphases]

What interests me particularly about this paragraph is its oscillation between expressions of self-depreciation and self-congratulation—the same oscillation or tension that we find compressed in the "minor female Wordsworth" epithet within it. Bishop, whose poetry was closely connected with and often inspired by her travels, admits that Lowell's planned European tour has her feeling "ugly and envious." That the question of envy is not disconnected from literary competition we feel in this correspondence, especially since

Lowell's new book, *The Mills of the Kavanaughs*, just out from Harcourt Brace, has been the chief topic of their recent letters.[3] Bishop turns in the paragraph from the humorously derogatory description of herself as "ugly and envious" to a listing of her own recent literary accomplishments: an article she hopes to publish in the *New Yorker*, her Lucy Martin Donnelly Fellowship from Bryn Mawr, her plans for her forthcoming book (eventually published, not as "Concordance" but as *A Cold Spring*, in 1955). Then, in another swing, comes an expression of self-doubt: the book has not "jelled" yet. Continuing with a disarmingly unambitious metaphor ("I'm only making jam here"), there is her slyly double-edged suggestion that the as yet unfinished portion of the manuscript may "prove to be pure pectin" (i.e., may bind the book together, but perhaps only with filler). Next, Bishop more confidently proffers the book's projected title. And, finally, she coins her provocative "minor female Wordsworth" appellation. Reading over her manuscript, with its many pentameter-based descriptive and meditative poems, Bishop has felt that of all her contemporaries (and perhaps Marianne Moore does not count as competition here, being a generation older than Bishop and Lowell), she is the greatest "Nature Lover," and therefore the most like Wordsworth. Habitually self-effacing, she avoids the embarrassing grandiosity of any claim to be a *modern* Wordsworth by tempering her comparison with the modifiers "minor" and "female," both of which in this context suggest the additional demure adverb, "merely." We may find the coyness of Bishop's phrasing—a kind of variation on "I'm just a girl"—irritating. (She herself seems self-conscious about this trace of stereotypic femininity, since she then jauntily swerves to the subject of an unapologetic "indelicacy" in one of her poems.) Yet, however humorously and hesitantly, Bishop *is* making a claim here for herself as chief "Nature Lover," or chief contemporary nature poet; even the words she uses ostensibly to undercut that claim may be read as not merely self-denigrating. Bishop's published and unpublished writing on the whole suggests that for her the "minor female" version is in some ways preferable to the "major male" prototype. Her wry self-description, then, is equivocal: disarmingly self-effacing as a public gesture, but expressive of private self-approval.

Bishop's dislike of selected Wordsworthian characteristics is evident in a passage from her early 1934–1936 journal:

> Wordsworth. "By My Sister"—keep all the honor for himself. All the "sirs." No sense of "drama." When does use of *This* OR *That* in titles date from? More useless than "and/or." Same sensation as Grandfather Bishop:
>
> 1. Looks?
> 2. Impossible to argue with, or to talk to, for (On the same vehicle, one wheel can revolve only as fast as another?)
> 3. just kept talking about LIFE, etc.
> 4. But chiefly: being sent on errands to a room full of strange *Presences*: electric Health Machine, models of bricks and samples of building materials, etc., liquor, books. "Powers" "Influences" (Attitude at time of his death towards Grandma, what M.F. said—very much like that of W's towards his sister.)[4]

Although these private notes remain frustratingly cryptic (Bishop was not, after all, writing with future literary critics in mind), they clearly display the young woman writer's annoyance and convey a sense of her partial identification with the original "minor female Wordsworth," another young "Nature Lover" who lived with a dominant male relation. Bishop's Wordsworth selfishly appropriates his sister Dorothy's journal observations;[5] like her own domineering paternal grandfather, he is opinionated and obstinate, and he holds forth endlessly and grandiloquently on the largest abstractions. In short, the young Bishop sees in Wordsworth another overbearing male, similar to the grandfather she describes in her memoir "The Country Mouse": "Now he descended, god-like and swearing, swept Grandma out of the way" (CPrEB, 13).

Of course, the very vehemence of Bishop's response to these prepotent male figures has its source in relatedness— in her literal kinship with her paternal grandfather, in her literary kinship with Wordsworth. And critics have already called attention to the significant ties between Bishop and her Romantic precursor. Robert Pinsky has shown how Bishop's project resembles Wordsworth's in having at its center "the contrast between the individual, single consciousness and the world not itself."[6] Willard Spiegelman has focused on the "Natural Heroism" in Bishop's poetry in an essay that explores "her kinship with, yet movement beyond, Wordsworth."[7] Keeping in mind Bishop's own terms for distinguishing herself from her predecessor, I would like to continue the discussion of that "movement beyond." How does this modern woman nature lover or nature poet move away from or beyond the "major male" poetry of Wordsworth? What, in this particular case at least, might a poetics of the "minor" and the "female" be?

Bishop's wonderfully intelligent and moving poetic production, we should acknowledge at the outset, eludes description as "major" in terms of its total size (the sum of her four slim volumes comparable to George Herbert's output rather than Wordsworth's). Bishop herself with regret attributes this lack of prolificness at least in part to her sex: "I know I wish I had written a great deal more. Sometimes I think if I had been born a man I probably would have written more. Dared more, or been able to spend more time at it. I've wasted a great deal of time."[8] Today, we might find the self-avowed timidity and procrastination of this woman writer explained as "anxiety of authorship."[9] Limited productivity can hardly be said to have been part of Bishop's poetic plan; yet there are ways in which her oeuvre may be seen as more purposefully "minor." Bishop's distaste for egocentricity and "major" philosophical volubility is apparent in her journal. Her extreme personal reticence makes the notion of an unabashedly autobiographical long poem, a Bishop *Prelude*, risible; her unrelenting skepticism makes presentation of any consoling poetic myth (such as that belief in the beneficent reciprocity between man and formative Nature which Harold Bloom calls Wordsworth's "Myth of Memory") unthinkable.[10] In a 1965 interview, Bishop explicitly states her disinterest in such large-scale undertakings:

> *Interviewer:* Do you think it is necessary for a poet to have a "myth"—Christian or otherwise—to sustain his work?
> *Miss Bishop:* It all depends—some poets do, some don't. The question, I must admit, doesn't interest me a great deal. I'm not interested in big-scale work as such. Something needn't be large to be good.[11]

Indeed, something large may be bad—as Bishop shows us in "Large Bad Picture." In this poem from her first book, Bishop describes a painted sunset in a manner that recalls—even self-consciously echoes—this famous passage from "Tintern Abbey":

>   And I have felt
> A presence that disturbs me with the joy
> Of elevated thoughts; a sense sublime
> Of something far more deeply interfused,
> Whose dwelling is the light of setting suns,
> And the round ocean and the living air,
> And the blue sky, and in the mind of man;
> A motion and a spirit, that impels
> All thinking things, all objects of all thought,
> And rolls through all things.[12]

"Magnificent," one feels that Bishop would say, "but untrue"—inaccurate to her own experience of spiritual isolation, and somehow fudging the issues in its grandly but vaguely phrased attempt at a cosmic blending or interfusion. Here are her own lines about the "Large Bad Picture"—simultaneously arch and wistful, ironic and nostalgic:

In the pink light
the small red sun goes rolling, rolling,
round and round and round at the same height
in a perpetual sunset, comprehensive, consoling

It would of course be wrong to posit Bishop's poem as simply a veiled response to, and partial parody of, Wordsworth. The more immediate and generous gesture of the poem is its affectionate re-creation of an actual family relic—a great-uncle's rather ordinary artistic production. Nevertheless, the "big picture" that Bishop describes— replete with sunset ("flushed, still sky") and cliffs ("overhanging pale blue cliffs/hundreds of feet high")—strongly evokes the familiar settings of Wordsworth's visionary experiences. And when we place this description next to "Poem," Bishop's homage in her final book to the same great-uncle's much smaller picture, our sense is reinforced that this poet is reflecting on her relation to the Romantic tradition of nature lovers through the vehicle of landscape painting.

In the early as well as the later poem, Bishop in a sense puts herself in the position of Dorothy, that other "minor female Wordsworth": she is like the young woman in "Tintern Abbey" in whom an older male relative's art and imagination continue to live. Here, though, the tables are turned. Bishop is not the silent receptacle of the "exhortations" of a brother two years older than she, but rather the speaking survivor of a dead great-uncle, two generations older. She is not the artless source and after-echo of her relative's accomplishment, but rather (as the craft with which Bishop describes her great-uncle's somewhat pedestrian paintings makes clear) the more accomplished artist.

Although some ironic distancing is at work in Bishop's treatment of both paintings, we also feel the empathic engagement of this poet (who produced occasional charming sketches and watercolors and who repeatedly said that she'd "love to be a painter")[13] with another artist's work. And this empathy is far more pronounced in the later poem about her great-uncle's much smaller piece. The painting described in "Poem" is artistically unremarkable, monetarily worthless, and miniscule ("about the size of an old-style dollar bill")—a distinctly minor work (a "minor family relic," just as Bishop is a "minor female Wordsworth"). Despite this apparent inconsequentiality—or rather because of it—Bishop identifies her own life and art with the "useless and free" family artifact she describes. The "old-style dollar bill" to which the tiny painting is likened shares Elizabeth Bishop's own uncertain "American or Canadian" nationality; the generic title "Poem" does not separate the observing poet from the painter, as does "Large Bad Picture," but instead invites association by analogy; and the greater length of this later work (exactly twice as many lines as "Large Bad Picture") manifests Bishop's greater affinity for her relative's small-scale production. What, then, can we say about Bishop's response to and implied revision of "major male" Romanticism in "Poem," her reprise (so to speak) of painting in the minor key?

> About the size of an old-style dollar bill,
> American or Canadian,
> mostly the same whites, gray greens, and steel grays
> —this little painting (a sketch for a larger one?)
> has never earned any money in its life.
> Useless and free, it has spent seventy years
> as a minor family relic
> handed along collaterally to owners
> who looked at it sometimes, or didn't bother to.

First, we can notice how Wordsworthian this poem actually is: all about the re-collection of experience through memory and art; about spontaneity in art (the small sketch "done in an hour, 'in one breath' "); about the love of nature; about looking or gazing; about capturing, in common speech, common life. Next, we can observe how

Bishop moves beyond Wordsworth by going him one better—or rather (since Bishop's revisionism is so often a matter of scaling down proportion and diminishing expectation) by going him one smaller.

Take, for example, the most self-conscious incidence of revision in "Poem." "Our visions coincided," Bishop writes (meaning that she and her great-uncle, though not contemporaries, have shared a view of the same spot)—but then, immediately, she corrects herself: " 'visions' is/too serious a word—our looks, two looks." This refusal of lofty diction ("lofty" itself a Wordsworthianism foreign to Bishop's vocabulary) is connected with other, larger refusals. When Bishop replaces the exalted "visions" with the matter-of-fact "looks," she turns with that small gesture from Romantic poetry, with its emphasis on soaring subjectivity, toward a modern poetry of more minutely observant objectivity.[14] She is readjusting the balance, one might say, between "I" and "eye."

> Five years have passed; five summers, with the length
> Of five long winters! and again I hear
> These waters, rolling from their mountain springs
> With a soft inland murmur.—Once again
> Do I behold these steep and lofty cliffs,
> That on a wild, secluded scene impress
> Thoughts of more deep seclusion; and connect
> The landscape with the quiet of the sky.

Wordsworth returns to a spot above Tintern Abbey, overlooking the valley of the river Wye, after an absence of five years, chiefly in order to review the stages of his own spiritual development and to reaffirm his "myth of memory"; and this subjective focus necessarily leads to a blurring of the immediate sensory world outside himself. We know that Wordsworth is seated under a "dark sycamore," but the rest of the scene (with the possible exception of the more closely observed and charmingly English "hedge-rows, hardly hedge-rows, little lines/Of sportive wood run wild") remains vaguely defined. Wordsworth surveys "these waters," "these steep and lofty cliffs," "these plots of cottage-ground," "these orchard-tufts" with general affection, but only with some uncertain notice. Bishop, in contrast, grateful for the chance to re-visit her childhood Nova Scotia village through her dead relative's small painting, honors his exact (if rather uninspired) record by verbally re-creating each daub: white and yellow wild iris, the Presbyterian church, Miss Gillespie's house. Looks have been substituted for "visions," physical observation for philosophical observations, the merely natural for the myth of Nature.

But "Tintern Abbey" is permanently poignant in the immensity of its wishfulness. "And so I dare to hope," the poet writes—and with language that hovers precariously between extremes of confirmation and negation (between "all" and "never," "no," "nor"), he creates a benevolent power, a prayer, and even his own blessing and answer to that prayer:

> Oh! yet a little while
> May I behold in thee what I was once,
> My dear, dear sister! and this prayer I make,
> Knowing that Nature never did betray
> The heart that loved her; 'tis her privilege,
> Through all the years of this our life, to lead
> From joy to joy; for she can so inform
> The mind that is within us, so impress
> With quietness and beauty, and so feed
> With lofty thoughts, that neither evil tongues,
> Rash judgments, nor the sneers of selfish men,
> Nor greetings where no kindness is, nor all
> The dreary intercourse of daily life,
> Shall e'er prevail against us, or disturb
> Our cheerful faith that all which we behold
> Is full of blessings. Therefore let the moon
> Shine on thee in thy solitary walk;
> And let the misty mountain-winds be free
> To blow against thee; and, in after years,

When these wild ecstasies shall be matured
Into a sober pleasure; when thy mind
Shall be a mansion for all lovely forms,
Thy memory be as a dwelling-place
For all sweet sounds and harmonies; oh! then,
If solitude, or fear, or pain, or grief,
Should be thy portion, with what healing thoughts
Of tender joy wilt thou remember me,
And these my exhortations!

After that boldness and grandeur—a grandeur haunted, one feels, by unspoken anxiety, and tinged as well with patriarchal condescension—here is Bishop's plain poetry of diminished expectation:

I never knew him. We both knew this place,
apparently, this literal small backwater,
looked at it long enough to memorize it,
our years apart. How strange. And it's still loved,
or its memory is (it must have changed a lot).
Our visions coincided—"visions" is
too serious a word—our looks, two looks:
art "copying from life" and life itself,
life and the memory of it so compressed
they've turned into each other. Which is which?
Life and the memory of it cramped
dim, on a piece of Bristol board,
dim, but how live, how touching in detail
—the little that we get for free,
the little of our earthly trust. Not much.
About the size of our abidance
along with theirs: the munching cows,
the iris, crisp and shivering, the water
still standing from spring freshets,
the yet-to-be-dismantled elms, the geese.

Decidedly not grand, this conclusion—with its halting rhythms, its colloquialisms, its diction of diminution ("small," "compressed," "cramped," "little"). And, although permeated by a melancholy and meditative intelligence, not "too serious." (What a difference in tone if we delete those quietly funny "munching cows," or choose to end the poem without those geese.) In a voice cautiously restrained—as though to indicate that the best defense against despair is not to "dare to hope" extravagantly, as Wordsworth does, but rather to hope for as little as possible (since so little seems possible)—Bishop expresses gratitude for the small miracle of coincident "looks." And that small miracle, with its attendant moment of recognition and pleasure (not any gift of "cheerful faith" or lasting solace) is all, the poet makes us feel, that nature or that her post-Romantic poetry has to offer.

She makes us feel this partly with her music—here, as I have just mentioned, a cautious, halting music, improvised off a pentameter base and patterned on paired verbal repetitions that express revisions or refinements of thought ("visions"/"visions"; "looks"/"looks"; "life"/ "life"; "little"/"little"). The clipped and chainstitched phrases make us start and stop and start again. Only in the last lines of her poem does she admit an easier, more eloquent extension (similar to Wordsworth's extensions by anaphora in "Tintern Abbey"):

> . . . the munching cows,
> the iris, crisp and shivering, the water
> still standing from spring freshets,
> the yet-to-be-dismantled elms, the geese.

But here she eschews sentimentality with humor and with the wry wit of "yet-to-be-dismantled." She undercuts poetic loft by cutting, in the penultimate line, the stately pentameter short.

This reluctance "to allow technical intensity and thematic passion to correspond in her work" has been pointed out by Penelope Laurans in an essay on Bishop's use of metrical variation.[15] According to Laurans, "Bishop exercises her technical proficiency to cut her poetry off from any of that 'spontaneous overflow of powerful feeling' so immediately central to the Romantic imagination."[16]

Especially at those infrequent moments when she approaches the grand style, such as in the sonorous conclusion of "At the Fishhouses," Bishop will deflate intensity by her technique:

> It is like what we imagine knowledge to be:
> dark, salt, clear, moving, utterly free,
> drawn from the cold hard mouth
> of the world, derived from the rocky breasts
> forever, flowing and drawn, and since
> our knowledge is historical, flowing, and flown.

Here the verse flirts with pentameter, but resists that stately regularity. The comparison (knowledge/seawater) is rather traditional and grand, but made at two cautious removes: "It is *like* what we *imagine*." The special emotional quality of Bishop's verse—lyrical but not effusive, plangent but not blaring—is largely, as Laurans' readings make clear, a matter of using metrical variation to mute the Romantic horn.

But with her metrical practices (practices influenced by her close acquaintance with George Herbert's mixed meters), Bishop may be responding to and revising "major male" poetry even more broadly. As A.R.C. Finch succinctly puts it in an article on the metrical strategies of Emily Dickinson, pentameter is the meter most closely associated with "the supremely subjective lyric 'I'—employed by men for centuries to appropriate the world, the world as woman—and woman."[17] On the one hand, Bishop is traditional in her attachment to this meter, used by Wordsworth before her to treat the subject of "the contrast between the individual single consciousness and the world not itself."[18] She herself acknowledges this conservatism in a letter to the more formally radical Marianne Moore: "I think my approach is so much vaguer and less defined and certainly more old-fashioned—sometimes I'm amazed at people's comparing me to you when all I'm doing is some kind of blank verse—can't they *see* how different it is?"[19] On the other hand, Bishop's deployments of metrical variation are revisionary: consistently refusing the regularity of pentameter (writing "some kind of blank verse"), she avoids alliance with a tradition of vaunting subjectivity and masculine appropriation. Although Bishop's eschewal of metrical regularity is perfectly in line with modernist male dicta ("To break the pentameter, that was the first heave," as Pound said),[20] her characteristic straddling of the metrical fence may best be understood as part of her "minor female" response to Wordsworthian Romanticism. In her formal decisions, then, Bishop would seem to resemble those nineteenth-century women writers whom Sandra Gilbert and Susan Gubar discuss—writers who found means "of achieving true female literary authority by simultaneously conforming to and subverting patriarchal literary standards."[21]

Consider, for example, Bishop's technique in another poem—the first in her first book. With "The Map," as I have suggested earlier, Bishop tells us that she conceives of her poetry as an act of mapmaking, the painstaking representation of the known world. Poetry, like a map, should provide "a description of the earth's surface." This phrase—part of the geography lessons from an 1884 textbook that serve as epigraph to Bishop's final book, *Geography III*—expresses concisely both this poet's ambition (she wants to take on the whole planet) and her humility (she can offer only a "description," not a creation or a vision; she can describe only the "surface"). In "The Map" Bishop finds a way to embody both attitudes through a subtly innovative, shifting form.

The iambic pentameter base is established with the first line ("Land lies in water; it is shadowed green"), but the succeeding lines only hover around pentameter, with a tetrameter line in the first stanza ("along the fine tan sandy shelf") and irregular, hypermetric lines mixed in with pentameter, particularly in the unrhymed middle stanza:

The names of seashore towns run out to sea,
the names of cities cross the neighboring mountains
—the printer here experiencing the same excitement
as when emotion too far exceeds its cause.
These peninsulas take the water between thumb and finger
like women feeling for the smoothness of yard-goods.

Here as elsewhere Bishop resists rhythmic predictability—
that tendency to which, as she once remarked in a letter to
Moore, Wallace Stevens occasionally capitulates, "to make
blank verse *moo.*"[22] Rhyme and meter emerge, disappear,
and reappear in a fashion that suggests both this poet's
desire to comprehend the world (to seize it with her own
mind) and that world's perpetual elusiveness.

With image and figure as well as meter, Bishop acknowledges the independence and elusiveness of the natural
world. She composes less intricate and strange analogies
than does Marianne Moore (Moore's "firs . . . each with
an emerald turkey-foot at the top" or her cat Peter, with
"shadbones regularly set about the mouth/to droop or rise
in unison like porcupine-quills"); but like her modern ex-
emplar Bishop shows both poetic ingenuity and respect for
irrepressible "otherness" by comparing creatures or objects
to other natural creatures or objects—as in these palm tree
similes from her first two books:

The palm trees clatter in the stiff breeze
like bills of pelicans.
                              ("FLORIDA")

The branches of the date-palms look like files.
("OVER 2000 ILLUSTRATIONS AND A COMPLETE
    CONCORDANCE")

Think of the boulevard and the little palm trees
all stuck in rows, suddenly revealed
as fistfuls of limp fish-skeletons.
                              ("LITTLE EXERCISE")

This is a variety of analogizing foreign to Wordsworth—
who, in promoting his grand theme of reciprocity or

interfusion, is more likely to compare human beings to birds or flowers, stars or clouds. Bishop's comparisons arise from her gratitude for the refreshment of the nonhuman, and she concentrates on seeing minutely and clearly, rather than on becoming a sublime seer. Even Bishop's characteristic choice of simile over the more confident trope of metaphor expresses her un-Wordsworthian sense of the limits of imagination. As Robert Pinsky points out in a review of Bishop's *Complete Poems,* the simile, which self-consciously posits connections between separate things, "qualifies the sublime, limiting how much can be known. . . . That a person can be known, or the intensely visible world understood, is always left partly in doubt."[23]

And doubt—so much a part of Bishop's poetry of constant self-correction, hesitation, interrogation—is precisely what Wordsworth's poetry attempts to debar. Out of the strength of his imagination and the splendor of his language, Wordsworth constructs his consoling myth or "cheerful faith"; and his poetry is all the more moving because we sense in it the just-suppressed suspicion that at any moment the top-heavy construction might collapse. Wordsworth proposes, as Harold Bloom puts it, "a marriage between the Mind of Man and the goodly universe of Nature."[24] He "never considers," as Bloom goes on to say, "the more sinister manifestation of Nature-as-temptress, Blake's Vala or Keats's Belle Dame."[25] He certainly never entertains the notion (which at the end of the nineteenth century becomes Thomas Hardy's obsession) that nature might be entirely indifferent to him. Wordsworth's myth depends upon the kindliness and fidelity of his bride—and he wills himself to believe that she will remain faithful: "Nature never did betray/The heart that loved her."

Wordsworth's love is unequivocal; but in the Wordsworthian marriage, the "Mind of Man," and not the "goodly universe of Nature," is ultimately the dominant partner—as the conclusion of his *Prelude* makes clear:

Prophets of Nature, we to them will speak
A lasting inspiration, sanctified
By reason, blest by faith: what we have loved,
Others will love, and we will teach them how;
Instruct them how the mind of man becomes
A thousand times more beautiful than the earth
On which he dwells, above this frame of things
(Which, 'mid all revolution in the hopes
And fears of men, doth still remain unchanged)
In beauty exalted, as it is itself
Of quality and fabric more divine.

(1850 VERSION)

Here, even as Wordsworth proclaims himself and Coleridge prophets of a new religion of nature, he establishes them as instructors in the old hierarchy. This stirring paean to the human imagination, then, is disturbingly patriarchal, particularly for the woman who aspires to "speak" herself, to be a writer: she has been led by the collective force of Wordsworth's spousal vision to see herself (together with the rest of her sex) as transcended "earth" or object, rather than transcendent subject.

Like Marianne Moore before her, Elizabeth Bishop (who considered herself "a strong feminist")[26] revises this gendered agenda, replacing the Romantic poet's resounding certainties with dubiety, doubleness, radical ambiguity. Throughout her work, she subverts the conventional Romantic trope of world-as-woman by insisting upon the indeterminate nature of nature—now female, now male, now ungendered other. And, as we might expect, Bishop is most subversive at her most Wordsworthian moments. In "The Fish," for example—strikingly Wordsworthian in its evocation of almost religious awe and joy in the presence of embodied nature—Bishop re-figures the usual Romantic figure, making us see nature as a "He," a sort of finny five-star general:

I admired his sullen face,
the mechanism of his jaw,

and then I saw
that from his lower lip
—if you could call it a lip—
grim, wet, and weaponlike,
hung five old pieces of fish-line,
or four and a wire leader
with the swivel still attached,
with all their five big hooks
grown firmly in his mouth.
A green line, frayed at the end
where he broke it, two heavier lines,
and a fine black thread
still crimped from the strain and snap
when it broke and he got away.
Like medals with their ribbons
frayed and wavering,
a five-haired beard of wisdom
trailing from his aching jaw.

But even as she develops her own alternative figure, Bishop holds it up to question. She introduces this fiercely independent, masculine version of the fish with a contrasting version—domestic, and (as a result of the poet's sly adaptation of the timeworn girls-as-flowers trope) suggestive of the feminine:

Here and there
his brown skin hung in strips
like ancient wallpaper,
and its pattern of darker brown
was like wallpaper:
shapes like full-blown roses
stained and lost through age.
He was speckled with barnacles,
fine rosettes of lime,
. . . .
and the pink swim-bladder
like a big peony.

Determinedly "unpoetic" in her prosy rhythms, her patient agglomeration of seemingly random details and associations, Bishop here avoids poetic presumption, subjective sway. She acknowledges the tenuous relation of figurative language to reality with the tentativeness of simile ("Like medals"; "shapes like full-blown roses"; "like a big peony"). Humorously, she undercuts her own anthropomorphism ("—if you could call it a lip—"). And with a pile-up of arresting particulars, she tips the scale toward quizzical observation rather than controlling allegory.

Nevertheless, Bishop's frequently anthologized "The Fish" gradually accrues more allegorical point than most of her poems (one reason why it is a teachers' favorite). It slowly builds, as I have already suggested, toward a more Wordsworthian—more emotionally rounded, end-rhymed, and almost visionary—conclusion:

> I stared and stared
> and victory filled up
> the little rented boat,
> from the pool of bilge
> where oil had spread a rainbow
> around the rusted engine
> to the bailer rusted orange,
> the sun-cracked thwarts,
> the oarlocks on their strings,
> the gunnels—until everything
> was rainbow, rainbow, rainbow!
> And I let the fish go.

In fact, this poem bears a strong resemblance to a particular Wordsworth poem, "Resolution and Independence," which also begins with refreshing directness ("There was a roaring in the wind all night"), describes a similarly graced encounter between the poet and some "natural" presence, and issues in a specific moral action.

Both poems are concerned, even obsessively, with the relation between exterior and interior life and with achieving moral understanding (never, in Bishop's case, the same thing as moralizing), but finally they commit themselves to opposite actions. Ranging over the landscape, taking it

into himself, Wordsworth essentially interiorizes. In "Resolution and Independence," everything the moody and meandering poet sees (brooding stock-dove, mirthful hare,
ancient leech-gatherer, muddy water) becomes assimilated
into his own mental state. It is no accident that the poem is
so strikingly Spenserian—evoking Spenser's figure of Despair, containing archaisms and syntactical inversions, and
composed in a kind of abbreviated Spenserian stanza
(rhyme royal with concluding alexandrines). For it is a
Romantic adaptation of allegory in which nature bodies
forth the individual poet's psychology—and that "man-
scape," not the landscape nor the old leech-gatherer within
it, is the real focus of attention. Almost entirely absorbed
back into nature, the leech-gatherer (feeble, stooped, and,
although masculine, rather crone-like) has been transmog-
rified into "a huge stone," "a sea-beast," "a cloud." An
iconic projection as much as a real presence, he appears to
Wordsworth "like one whom I had met with in a dream."
In one way about the transformation wrought upon the
poet by his unexpected meeting with a strange and separate existence, Wordsworth's great poem is also about the
preemptive mind's ultimate solipsistic self-engagement:
"While I these thoughts within myself pursued."[27] The
title refers at once to the leech-gatherer's resolution (his
determined activity and philosophical settlement with his
situation) and to Wordsworth's final resolution to hold in
memory, in his "mind's eye," the whole restorative emblematic arrangement; it underscores, then, not only the
spectral figure's independence (his self-reliance and isolation) but also the poet's imaginative self-sufficiency and
self-absorption.

Bishop avoids Wordsworth's egocentric, centripetal action by externalizing, focusing outward, as the title of her
poem tells us, on "The Fish." Whereas Wordsworth inter-
nalizes and subsumes a naturalized human being (the almost moss-covered leech-gatherer), Bishop attends to a
separate, natural creature: first by "catching" the fish both

literally and figuratively (by hooking it and simultaneously "capturing" it with self-conscious anthropomorphic comparisons), and then by letting the fish—together with any suggestion of co-optive figuration—go. Her perceptions lead not merely to imaginative conquest or introspection, but to a sense of mutual "victory" and a specific action. She saves the creature's life. The undeniably serious conclusion with its Noah's Ark-like rainbow still has about it her very quiet, and very un-Wordsworthian, touch of humor (in what is, after all, a kind of elaborate "fish story"). And it suggests a sense of social exchange and respectfulness that reminds one not of Wordsworth, but again of George Herbert. The final line with its initial conjunction—"And I let the fish go"—in fact resembles some of the well-mannered actions, or polite requests for divine action, at the conclusions of Herbert's (also short-lined, also cannily "child-like") poems: "And mend my rhyme"; "And heal my troubled breast which cryes,/Which dyes"; "And I reply'd *My Lord*"; "So I did sit and eat."

Agnostic and nostalgic, Bishop of course adopts neither Herbert's Christian faith nor his filial and courtly relation with God. Rather, she adapts (in "The Fish" and elsewhere) his social, dramatically interactive version of religious life for her own more secular—but still importantly spiritual—experience. Her poetry, as Willard Spiegelman points out, characteristically stresses exchange and empathy, as opposed to Wordsworthian egoism and epiphany: "Where Bishop surpasses Wordsworth . . . where her egoism is simply less intense, is in her continual insistence on the need for symbiosis: mutual support, rather than epiphanies wrought by otherworldly visitors, is the key to natural polity, as well as piety."[28] Making explicit what is perhaps implicit ln Spiegelman's essay, I would say that Bishop's less egocentric, more respectfully attentive relation to nature and natural creatures stems directly from her identity as a woman writer and is part of her "minor female" revision of Wordsworthian Romanticism.

What Bishop is working against, as I have already mentioned, is the traditional Romantic conflation, and concomitant male domination, of woman and nature. She resists this conventional association by undermining fixed gender attribution within particular poems (such as "The Fish") and by destabilizing the sexual nature of nature throughout her work as a whole—portraying, for example, "The Fish" as male (with some complicating "feminine" properties), the big, bus-stopping creature in "The Moose" as female, and "The Weed" as ungendered but powerfully manipulative "other." By frequently personifying such natural entities, she suggests their coequality with humans. By consistently questioning or undercutting her own personifications, she acknowledges the natural world's independence from human concepts and concerns—its essential, and almost magical, strangeness. These are very wily movements of the mind, by which Bishop distinguishes herself from nature (in order to write about it), even as she demonstrates solidarity, so to speak, with that other member of the Resistance. In response to the Romantic poet's two-fold domination, we might say then that Bishop claims not alikeness with nature, but a kind of uneasy—even paradoxically combative—alliance.

And we see this same resistance to domination in her portraits of human as well as nonhuman subjects. When describing male characters or adopting male personae, Bishop sidesteps the usual sexual hierarchy and debunks myths of masculine heroism and conquest.[29] Her Gentleman of Shalott, for example, supposing himself half-absorbed into Tennyson's lady's mirror, is not militant but modest, not doughty but doubtful, not superhuman but silly—a long way from the legendary Sir Lancelot. Her Man-Moth, weird amalgam of man and nature (or natural creature), not only embodies this poet's poignant feeling of anomalousness, but also reverses the traditional Romantic association of woman and nature and controverts conventional heroism with his uncertainty and timidity, then his

one slyly palmed tear. And Crusoe, her most complex
male persona, is, among other things, an ironic diminish-
ment of Defoe's resourceful, practical, self-reliant and self-
assured hero.

Bishop's Crusoe is hypersensitive and indecisive, prone
to error, humble about his ignorance—and frankly plain-
tive:

> I often gave way to self-pity.
> "Do I deserve this? I suppose I must.
> I wouldn't be here otherwise. Was there
> a moment when I actually chose this?
> I don't remember, but there could have been."
> What's wrong about self-pity, anyway?
> With my legs dangling down familiarly
> over a crater's edge, I told myself
> "Pity should begin at home." So the more
> pity I felt, the more I felt at home.

With her wryly funny, certainly not "macho," alternative
to Defoe's sturdy, eighteenth-century pragmatist, Bishop
manages to conform to nineteenth-century Romantic values and to undo them as well. On the one hand, she demonstrates her own literary and historical connection with
Romanticism by making her Crusoe more sensitive to natural phenomena, more introspective, more emotionally vul-
nerable and expressive than Defoe's original. On the other
hand, by selecting as her persona this shipwrecked sailor, ir-
remediably and painfully isolated in bleak, unyielding nature (a nature modeled, one might note in passing, on her
own perception of the dismaying, goat-populated desola-
tion of Aruba),[30] Bishop ironizes Wordsworth's consoling
myth of responsive, nurturing Nature. With her ironically
incompleted quotation from "I Wandered Lonely as a
Cloud," she punctures her Romantic predecessor's inflated
notion of "the bliss of solitude":

> The books
> I'd read were full of blanks;

the poems—well, I tried
reciting to my iris-beds,
"They flash upon that inward eye,
which is the bliss . . ." The bliss of what?
One of the first things that I did
when I got back was look it up.

Bishop's conflicted, sometimes yearning relation to Romanticism is expressed not only through her allusive and stereotype-elusive male characters, but also through characters who more obviously resemble Wordsworth's creations—the perceptive young children of "First Death in Nova Scotia" and "In the Waiting Room," whose nineteenth-century prototypes we find in the *Lyrical Ballads*. (This literary historical kinship is underscored in both Bishop poems by her use of short, mostly three-beat free verse lines, which resemble the short lines of Wordsworth's ballads.)[31] In keeping with the cherished Romantic notion that small children are especially wise or insightful—but at the same time in resistance to the Romantic emphasis on children's blessedness and happiness—Bishop's grave young personae are more awake to the weirdness and perilousness of the human condition than the adults around them. The quizzical, apprehensive small child in "First Death in Nova Scotia" does not share, for example, the immunity to grief and obliviousness to loss that characterize the "simple child" in Wordsworth's parable of wise innocence, "We Are Seven." And the almost-seven-year-old Elizabeth in "In the Waiting Room" experiences not a Wordsworthian sense of cosmic embrace, but rather the alternating terrors of a centripetal force that squashes her together with other people (her aunt, whose scream "from inside" seems to be her own, the woman in the *National Geographic Magazine* with "awful hanging breasts") along with a centrifugal force that threatens to spin her off "into cold, blue-black space."

As the emphasized name later in the poem makes clear,

the precocious female minor in "In the Waiting Room"—
with her sensitivity to language and interest in reading, her
acute powers of observation and her anxiety about growing up a woman—is a prefiguration of the adult poet or
"minor female Wordsworth." Elizabeth Bishop looks back
in this poem (in what will be her final book) on her anxious
and overwhelmed child self with still-fresh empathy, but
with the assurance and control of the accomplished artist.
She has by this time fulfilled the self-assigned task of
making a space for herself as a woman writer, particularly
as a female "Nature Lover" with significant ties to Wordsworthian Romanticism. Because this nineteenth-century
tradition strongly links woman to nature, and so tends
toward the objectification of women, Bishop like Marianne Moore has discovered certain means of challenging
that conventional association. She has (again, like Moore)
resisted the Romantic poet's domination of woman and
nature by diminishing masculine notions of conquest and
by refusing to engage, herself, in imaginative imperialism.

Bishop's small but eloquent body of work at once extends the life of the Romantic tradition and tries to lay some
of its tendencies to rest—a double action that seems to be
figuratively encapsulated in some lines from *Geography III*.
One might, for example, see her Crusoe's Island—"a sort of
cloud-dump"—as a refuse heap of (cloud- and mist-filled)
Wordsworthian poetry, and perhaps the island's many wa-
terspouts, with "their heads in cloud," as ghosts of Romantic poets. Reading "Five Flights Up," the last poem in this
final volume, one might imagine Bishop glancing both
ironically and nostalgically at the outworn fantasy of her
(nightingale-, thrush-, and skylark-obsessed) Romantic
forebears with her own "unknown bird," which "seems to
yawn." And finally, reading the last line of this poem—"(A
yesterday I find almost impossible to lift.)"—one might
think of Bishop as commenting not only upon the accumu-
lated burden of personal consciousness, but also upon the

almost overwhelming Romantic literary inheritance. From this perspective, she would seem to be acknowledging Wordsworthian Romanticism as an enormous achievement, an oppressive force—and yet a not-quite-insurmountable challenge.

5 ·
Literary Models, Maternity, and Paternity

IN THE PREVIOUS CHAPTERS I HAVE explored, through attention to selected poems, Moore's and Bishop's relations to the two English literary periods that most forcefully impinged upon American modernism. Both women, like so many of their male contemporaries, took for their models seventeenth-century writers in lieu of the nineteenth-century poets widely associated, at least from Pound on, with formal predictability, mawkishness, imprecision, and mannerism. However, the patterns of persistence and resistance, filiation and rebellion, that we find in the work of these two writers distinguish them in a noticeable way from their (first- and second-generation modernist) male peers. Despite marked differences between Moore's and Bishop's individual stylistic and thematic practices, these two women writers, as earlier chapters have suggested, nevertheless resemble one another in their complex attitudes toward nature and in their canny methods of indirection—in their mutual adoption of what might be called a policy of enabling humility.

Why, though, one might speculate further, did these

two poets choose the particular late Renaissance models they chose, and what do these choices indicate about their individual relations to modernist problems and programs? Finally, how do Moore's and Bishop's uses of the English literary tradition contribute to or complicate the notion of a female tradition in literature?

Moore's interest in Sir Thomas Browne and other seventeenth-century prose writers had begun in adolescence and was enduring. The young poet clearly felt kinship with Browne's latitudinarian Protestantism (she wrote "relig." in the margin of her Bryn Mawr notes next to entries on Browne); she was at home with his Christian humility and his humor, his quirkiness and insatiable natural curiosity. Browne possessed in writerly fullness certain characteristics that Moore had also imbibed from her most influential friend and companion, her mother: deep religious feeling, a delight in wielding a precise and priceless vocabulary, a penchant for astonishing syntactical feats.[1] At the same time, he provided her (it is my guess) with an appealingly odd, yet undeniably successful, safe and sane artistic parent—a sort of literary replacement for the father she had lost even before birth to failure and mental imbalance. Founded in familial values and obsessions, and dating at least from her 1909 course in imitative prose, Moore's strong attraction to Browne was clearly an expression of personal predilections predating by several years Pound's call for "a renaissance, or awakening" in letters,[2] as well as predating, of course, Eliot's enormously influential 1921 essay on seventeenth-century metaphysical poets.

Still, Moore's interest in the Renaissance, to which so many modernists were drawn, cannot be chalked up to mere personal coincidence. The English seventeenth century offered a pattern—and, by association, a promise—of literary renewal, breathtaking authorial competence and confidence. Besides, it had all the charm for a twentieth-century poet of distance—being associated neither with the almost overwhelming potency and ensuing embarrassing enfeeblement of the nineteenth-century-as-parent, nor with the claustrophobic formality and brittleness of the eighteenth-century-as-grandparent. It seemed, finally, a kind of fountain of literary health, proffering a cure for inherited blights and sometimes apparently contradictory imbalances: chief among these, the felt primacy in nineteenth-century poetry of abstraction over concretion; mushy feeling over clear, hard thinking; of subjectivity over objectivity.

Like others of her generation, Moore was invigorated by the challenge, ambitious to right these perceived wrongs. Like many other American modernists—she answered when queried by Bishop about her earliest poetry that it was *"just* like Swinburne, Elizabeth" (CPrEB, 145)—Moore had begun by composing rhymed verses with a Pre-Raphaelite flavor, such as this delicately sensual, vaguely medievalistic verse, published in 1908 when she was a college junior in Bryn Mawr's *Tipyn o' Bob:*[3]

To My Cup-bearer

A lady or a tiger-lily,
Can you tell me which,
I can see her when I wake at night
Incanting, like a witch.
Her eye is dark, her vestment rich
Embroidered with a silver stitch,
A lady or a tiger-lily,
Slave, come tell me which?

Using her familiarity with Browne and other Renaissance writers—seventeenth-century models other than those whose credentials for modernism were later proclaimed by Eliot—she formulated over the next decade her own insistently individual, inimitable modernist method. (One thinks here of the assertive independence of Moore's refusal of the imagist label, and of her wry rejoinder to Williams's depiction of her as a sort of supportive Mother-of-Modernists—a "saint" or red-headed "rafter": "I never was a rafter holding up anyone!").[4] Hers is an extreme objectivist poetry, delighting in the most microscopic, often thematically "irrelevant" detail; yet it makes room, as we have seen, for traditional Christian emblematizing and strong moral statement. A passage from *Religio Medici* that Moore marked in her 1931 Everyman's Library edition of Browne's writings points up similar impulses—toward the specific and the summarizing, the scientific and sermonic, the minuscule and the moral—in her seventeenth-century source:

> Indeed, what Reason may not go to School to the wisdom of Bees, Ants, and Spiders? What wise hand teacheth *them* what Reason cannot teach *us*? Ruder heads may stand amazed at those prodigious pieces of Nature, Whales, Serpents, Dromidaries and Camels; these, I confess, are the Colossus and majestic pieces of her hand; but in these narrow Engines there is more curious Mathematicks; and the civility of these little Citizens more neatly sets forth the Wisdom of their Maker.[5]

As the title of her second book suggests (her first book, entitled simply *Poems*, had been put together in England by her friends H.D. and Bryher), it was Moore's ambition to accommodate both large-scale and small-scale, philosophical and physical "Observations." Responding to the vexed relation between mind and world with a sort of modernist modulation of Sir Thomas Browne's ethical empiricism, her poetry achieves a singular and difficult balance. As Bonnie Costello writes:

> What distinguishes Moore from several other modernists of her period is the balance she achieves between representational and allegorical objectives. William Carlos Williams waged a war on symbols and clung to the particular. Wallace Stevens, on the other hand, took the symbol further into abstraction than any previous American artist. His images seem to belong almost completely to the imagination. Moore's poetry shares features of both, and retains a didactic element sometimes avoided in the early formalist phase of modernism. But here is

a modern didacticism, that will not divide message from medium.[6]

Moore's poetry, then, shares features of both Williams' and Stevens', even as it finally differs from theirs in its always compelling, if sometimes confusing, equality of image and imagination. It is also both like and unlike the poetry of Eliot and Pound—in ways that once again reflect the force of Moore's seventeenth-century prose models. Like Pound and Eliot, Moore combines elements of European traditionalism with American innovation and insurrection. But for Eliot's fatigue and sometime lugubriousness she substitutes a Renaissance-like energetic optimism, the quality that (adopting Hazlitt's term) she dubbed "gusto." The twentieth century did not unnerve but rather excited her; her response was not withdrawal but rather engagement. For Pound's secular complexes of myth and history—organizing principles of a poetics that often seems an awesome effort to reinvigorate literature and life by re-masculinizing them—she substitutes in her nonepic poetry unifying and affirming Christian faith.

When Moore, like her American contemporaries, broke from traditional meter, she invented poetic forms that seek to accommodate both things and her thinking about them, both her digressive and directive impulses.[7] Except for a brief period of free-verse experimentation (1920–1925), Moore composed for the most part in syllabic stanzas of varying strictness. These visually tidy stanzas (varying from poem to poem much like Herbert's stanzaic patterns) support the weight of her detail-and-quotation-encrusted, Renaissance-rich sentences, even as—with odd linebreaks and wordbreaks—they interrupt the flow of natural speech, self-consciously and modernistically holding linguistic elements up for display. Moore's capacious, often deliberately digressive poetic adaptation of Renaissance prose makes room for the autonomous and recalcitrant physical world she describes, while her crisp visual effects and grammatical precision are evidence of a modernist "hardness" and "neatness" of the mind that orders multifarious experience with élan.

Moore was Elizabeth Bishop's most important connection with the first generation of American modernists—a literary presence even before she became a friend, who made a life in poetry seem possible to the ambitious but still uncertain Vassar student. In a 1954 retrospective letter to Moore, Bishop writes: ". . . when I began to read your poetry at college I think it immediately opened up my eyes to the possibility of the subject-matter I could use and might never have thought of using if it hadn't been for you. —(I might not have written any poems at all, I suppose.)"[8] Bishop had in fact already written poems before she read or met Marianne Moore (although she might not, as a mature poet, have thought of them as "counting"). She had written, for example, a rhymed tetrameter lyric that echoes early Yeats ("Behind Stowe"), and a rather nineteenth-century melancholic "Sonnet." The year before she met Moore she completed her self-consciously Hopkinsesque "Three Sonnets for the Eyes":

> . . . See
> Flesh-forests, nerve-vined, pain-star-blossom full,
> Trackless to where trembles th'ears' eremite.

What Bishop's promising but not very successful imitative efforts have in common—what they adumbrate in the adult poet—is a kind of dramatic/descriptive tendency, a physicalizing or *visualizing* of psychology that Moore quickly located in her new protégée's work and praised as her capacity for "exteriorizing the interior."[9]

This obsessive interplay between psychology and sight, internal and external, is symbolically, sweetly, embodied in one of the best of Bishop's youthful efforts, written when she was sixteen:

To a Tree

Oh, tree outside my window, we are kin,
  For you ask nothing of a friend but this:
To lean against the window and peer in
  And watch me move about! Sufficient bliss

For me, who stand behind its framework stout,
  Full of my tiny tragedies and grotesque grieves,
To lean against the window and peer out,
  Admiring infinites'mal leaves.

The somewhat forced rhyme of "framework stout" and the sentimental and romanticized anthropomorphizing of the tree as "friend" are unlike the mature poet. (Bishop would later, in "Roosters," undercut both personification and sentimentality with the self-conscious simile, "faithful as enemy, or friend.") But the way the first stanza breaks elegantly after "Sufficient bliss," with that phrase then balanced humorously and poignantly by "grotesque grieves," reminds us of later moments in Bishop's work (when her "Gentleman of Shalott" remarks " 'Half is enough,' " for instance, or when Crusoe slyly indulges his self-pity in "Crusoe in England"). Most importantly, we glimpse in this youthful poem, which intriguingly resembles Robert Frost's "Tree at My Window,"[10] something of what nature was, and would remain, for Bishop: an entity distinct from herself, yet somehow related to her; an occasion for poetry and a means for meditation. More particularly, nature for her was a presence, encountered primarily through the sense of sight, which when contemplated carefully enough could lead one not only—predictably—back to the self and its troubles (the way the phrase "infinites'mal leaves" leads one back to "tiny tragedies"), but also—refreshingly, healingly—away from stale and self-critical introspection (the way that this early poem leaves Bishop and her reader not with contemplation of "grotesque grieves" but with admiring absorption in each minute leaf of the tree).

Given her own habit of connecting visible things with invisible thoughts and feelings, and given her profound gratitude for the natural world's inexhaustible and relieving (*almost* saving) otherness, it is no wonder that the young Elizabeth Bishop was immediately and powerfully drawn to Moore's poetry. Here was confirmation of many of her own (as yet rather uncertainly expressed) poetic instincts. Here, too, in Moore's coolly accomplished, bold, sometimes almost freakish extension of physical description— "feats of description," as Bishop admiringly observed, "beyond Hopkins' "— was a method for "stiffening" or modernizing her own Romantic tendencies.[11] One senses also that Moore's brisk objectivity must have seemed attractive "armor" to the shy, proud young woman who avoided vulgar (and painful) self-revelation—and who, early in her writing career, shielded herself with versions of Hopkins's dizzying, almost dotty, word puzzling, or with continental surrealism and Herbertian fantasticality.

Under Moore's mentorship, which included constant, companionable criticism, Bishop flourished, developing her descriptive capacities in letters to her new friend as well as in a burst of short stories and poems.[12] Efforts composed during the early years of this friendship, such as "The Imaginary Iceberg," "Paris, 7 A.M.," and "Florida," in their exuberant release of rather depersonalized descriptive energy seem undeniably "influenced" by Moore. (Moore especially approved of "The Imaginary Iceberg," which concludes with a somewhat Mooreish, somewhat moral and emblematic reference to "the soul.")[13] And in Bishop's final book we see a mature assimilation of Moore's work that goes far beyond mere "imitation"—in the syntactic extensions and the almost miraculously detailed observations of "The Moose," for example, or in this memorably odd moment of self-parodic, extreme descriptive fastidiousness in "The End of March":

my crypto-dream-house, that crooked box
set up on pilings, shingled green,
a sort of artichoke of a house, but greener
(boiled with bicarbonate of soda?)

If Moore's subject matter aided Bishop's artistic confidence and development—as she later gratefully acknowledged in her letter—it could not, of course, be identical with her own subject matter. Bishop's was a more skeptical and quizzical nature, and her bent was not for the sure counterpointing of moral and physical "Observations," but rather, as I have said, for the gentler interplay of introspection and extrospection, psychology and sight. She could not allow Moore's somewhat prudish sense of literary propriety (Moore's objection, for example, to the use of the phrase "water-closet" in "Roosters") or her mentor's well-meaning call for greater literary expression of "significant values" to censor or hamper her own talent.[14] Moore was quick to perceive her protégée's difference from herself, but she could not bring herself entirely to approve. "I do feel," she wrote to Bishop in May of 1938, "that tentativeness and interiorizing are your danger as well as your strength."[15]

"Tentativeness and interiorizing": Moore's apt phrase describes not only her protégée's proclivities, but tendencies of Bishop's seventeenth-century model as well. If what Bishop took from Moore was primarily development of her own talent for extrospection, for seeing accurately and describing with almost hallucinatory clarity, what she took from George Herbert were tools for poetic introspection, for the dramatic portrayal of psychological struggle and change. As shown earlier, reading side by side two poems that Bishop clearly indicated were indebted to Herbert ("The Weed" and "In the Waiting Room"), one sees first a fascinating and ingenious, if still somewhat apprenticelike imitation, and then a brilliantly assured original adaptation. Although Herbert is among the most devout of English poets, his work makes room for religious conflict, for evocation of an orthodox Christian's often troubled interior. In Elizabeth Bishop's work or "world"—so much darker, dreamier, and more uncertain than Marianne Moore's brightly lit world of insistent optimism and unwavering Christian faith—we find lyrics that, like Herbert's, record not only experiences of wonder and renewal, but also feelings of spiritual disorder and disempowerment, rebellion and homesickness. And Bishop's more skeptical poetry of psychological exploration adopts the childlike simplicity of tone, the questioning, and even the occasional querulousness that we associate with Herbertian speakers. Finally, Bishop's modern version of Herbert's seventeenth-century meditative poetry manages to be discretely revealing without being "confessional" in the manner of her autobiographically obsessed contemporary and close friend, Robert Lowell.[16]

Both Moore and Herbert, then, appealed to Bishop's natural reticence, and together they helped her fulfill the goal she had set for herself in her 1934 journal, to incorporate poetic content at once "material" and "spiritual." But Bishop's negotiation of formal problems, it seems to me, owes more to her seventeenth-century than to her twentieth-century model. Some formal features of Bishop's writing may show Moore's influence: the use of qualifying or complicating descriptive asides set off by parentheses or dashes, for instance, or a general tendency toward stanzaic neatness. But the latter is a feature of Herbert's writing as well—and Bishop had a more Herbert-like fondness for true rhymes (which Moore generally eschewed, pronouncing them "dowdy");[17] for traditional forms (the sonnet, with which Herbert's writing career had begun, as well as the villanelle, sestina, and ballad); and for short lines and mixed accentual meters. Most significantly, Bishop's forms resemble Herbert's—and differ from Moore's—in general structural conception. As John Ashbery has said, "The two poets couldn't be more different; Miss Moore's synthesizing, collector's approach is far from Miss Bishop's linear, exploring one."[18] Just as Moore's "collector's approach" displays the influence of her Renaissance prose models and suits her aims as both naturalistic and moralistic observer, so Bishop's "linear, exploring" structures show her adapting Herbert and other metaphysicals for her own modern and meditative poetic project.

The useful seventeenth-century parson and poet who had appeared to Bishop in her youthful dream remained, as her dream had somewhat equivocally suggested, a source unsurpassed by Marianne Moore. Yet Moore—whom Bishop many years later still associated, "like Alice, 'in a dreamy sort of way,' " with "mother; manners; morals" (CPrEB, 156)—is named in the dream, and so insistently juxtaposed to the feminine figure of Herbert, with "curls" and "wearing a beautiful dark red satin coat." We might say that Bishop's early dream vision conjures up and compares two maternal figures, the two poetic "mothers" at the intersection of whose powerful influences Bishop's unique contribution to modern American poetry may be located.

George Herbert, however, was not, of course, a woman writer, not what has come to be known as a literary "foremother." And this vexed and currently much-discussed issue of precursors and parentage, literary maternity and literary paternity, provokes a few observations.

THESE CHAPTERS HAVE BEEN CONCERNED with the phenomenon of literary influence—influence not merely as conscious or unconscious imitation and allusiveness, but rather as the poet's more complicated and subtly integrated response to her literary predecessors. I have been interested in what may be gained by reading Moore's and Bishop's poetry as both serious conversation with and strategic conversion of the work of their most significant Renaissance and Romantic precursors, and I have located in the poetry of each intricately intertwined affinities, affiliations, and oppositions. Such an intertextual approach, with concomitant attention to authorial relationships, is in fundamental agreement with Harold Bloom's stated understanding of the general task of literary criticism: "Criticism teaches not the language of criticism . . . but a language of influence, of the dialectic that governs the relation of poets *as poets*."[19]

Yet, as many critics, and especially feminist critics, have pointed out, Bloom's particular agonistic account of "the dialectic that governs the relation of poets *as poets*"—based as it is on a Freudian model of male psychological development—is inapt for female writers. Bloom, who describes his own 1973 theoretical book *The Anxiety of Influence* as "a severe poem," may see himself as participating in the literary historical drama there presented, the "battle between strong equals, father and son as mighty opposites, Laius and Oedipus at the crossroads," but there is no part for a woman writer in this all-male slice of Sophoclean drama.[20] Reading *The Anxiety*, with its story of nascent "strong poets" (or "ephebes") who must clear imaginative space for themselves through creative misreading (or "misprision"), and who must "wrestle with their strong precursors, even to the death,"[21] one may be reminded of the vision of a modern poet much admired and much written about by Bloom:

> Supple and turbulent, a ring of men
> Shall chant in orgy on a summer morn
> Their boisterous devotion to the sun,
> Not as a god, but as a god might be,
> Naked among them, like a savage source.[22]

Bloom's critical vision of burly male self-expression and self-assertion, like Stevens' stunning poetic one, might well prompt in a female reader and writer a kind of quizzical bemusement: "What men or gods are these?" she might ask, echoing yet another precursor. And it might bring to mind as well the less than dignified image of a well-fed Wallace Stevens—or, for that matter, of a white and attenuated T. S. Eliot—each stripped, oiled, and wrestling on a mat with his father-precursor(s) in some spot in eternity.

In fairness, it should be pointed out that Bloom has claimed for his theory "descriptive rather than prescriptive" status.[23] His own practice of antithetical criticism—deriving from Freud and Vico, the Kabbalah and Nietzsche—has produced discerning readings which have served as models for other literary critics (including feminist critics). And in the 1986 compilation of writings on *American Women Poets*, which he edited, Bloom in his introduction sensitively and sensibly considers the possibility that "the strongest women poets can possess: 'Another way — to see.' "[24]

Still, Bloom's influential theory of influence has bequeathed to feminist critics a seemingly ineluctable question: however adequate or inadequate *The Anxiety* may be as an account of what has been called the "patriarchal tradition," what would be (or, can there be) an adequate theoretical account of women writers' relation to their literary predecessors? I have not so far directly addressed this larger issue. Many of my own observations in these chapters have been minutely focussed—rather like those of Bishop's preoccupied "Sandpiper" whose "beak is focussed; . . . /looking for something, something, something." But in these concluding pages, I would like to consider my discussion of Moore and Bishop in the broader context of some of the most influential American feminist writing relevant to my subject of the uses of tradition. How might my detailed study of Moore's and Bishop's poetic practices variously conform to, conflict with, or in any way extend contemporary thinking about women writers' relation to the male-dominated or "patriarchal" tradition, or to what has been described as an autonomous and burgeoning "women's tradition?"

In many ways, these poets themselves—as their belated

and somewhat uneasy incorporation into the feminist critical canon suggests—resist enlistment into the ranks of a separate "women's tradition." Although Moore was central in many ways to Bishop's literary development, George Herbert was the younger poet's first, and lasting, model. It might be argued, then, that neither Bishop's nor Moore's *primary* literary model was a woman.[25] Neither poet was anxious to be grouped with other women writers. Elizabeth Bishop, in fact, adamantly refused to be so grouped, and remarked on her distaste for "women's anthologies" in her interview with George Starbuck:

> When I was in college and started publishing, even then, and in the following few years, there were women's anthologies, and all-women issues of magazines, but I always refused to be in them. I didn't think about it very seriously, but I felt it was a lot of nonsense, separating the sexes. I suppose this feeling came from feminist principles, perhaps stronger than I was aware of.[26]

In a 1977 letter to Joan Keefe, Bishop further explained her resistance on this point: "Undoubtedly gender does play an important part in the making of any art, but art is art and to separate writings, paintings, musical compositions, etc., into two sexes is to emphasize values in them that are *not* art."[27]

Bishop's quarrel is not with feminism, but rather with the practice—inimical to her own brand of feminism—of separating or segregating art according to gender. She finds this practice objectionable because it tends to emphasize the gender-linked social values that play a part in art's genesis, while overlooking the aesthetic qualities that distinguish one final artistic product from another. These are not, it seems to me, negligible reservations: American feminist literary criticism *has* tended to emphasize common female experience over individual aesthetic achievement, while on the whole encouraging sexual separation and polarization.

To study Bishop's, or Marianne Moore's, use of tradition is to observe bewilderingly complicated overlappings and intersections of various "influences": English and American; Renaissance, Romantic, and modern; scientific and spiritual; male and female. It is to see how an individually invented artistic stance may baffle any attempt at neat categorization under the rubric of "matriarchal" or "patriarchal." What had seemed (from the grand height of theory) two clearly distinct strands of literary parentage, upon close observation are inextricably intertwined. In saying this, I do not mean to ignore or erase the reality of gendered human experience, but rather to suggest that any inquiry into writing, particularly the writing of poetry, as a gendered experience must take into account the ever-changing and difficult-to-pinpoint activities of transmutation and transformation within, as Keats would have it, "the wreath'd trellis of a working brain." For example, surely the Herbert read and used by a poet at age fourteen is not the same Herbert read and used by that same poet at age thirty-five, forty-five; personal features in a literary ancestor are not only identified and analyzed by the poet's conscious and reasoning mind, but are intuited, projected, altered, fragmented, and sometimes recombined with features of other writers. The mind has no difficulty experiencing such a forerunner as male and fatherly sometimes, but female and motherly at other times—not to mention the possibilities of experiencing conflations and mazelike sibling rivalries that can participate with a living poet's life from the pages of a book.

If in these discussions it is also relevant, even required, to identify one's own feminist critical position, I would say that while I take seriously Bishop's objections to literary segregation of the sexes, I do not agree with her apparent refusal to consider directly the ways in which issues of gender may be linked to specific aesthetic practices—to artistic praxis as well as provenance. As Margaret Homans's study of women poets demonstrates, and as I have tried to show in these chapters, we can sometimes better perceive and appreciate particular aesthetic strategies by understanding their relation to "female experience," particularly if we acknowledge what Homans points out: that for a woman *poet* (of the nineteenth century, and still of Moore's and Bishop's generations) what may contribute most to the shaping of her art is "literary experience, the experience of reading poetry written almost exclusively by men."[28] My own position, then, lies between Bishop's more skeptical dismissal of gender as a literary issue, and the sex-focussed (often Sex-War-focussed) discussions of American feminist critics. In the paragraphs that follow I will briefly address four of the most well known and often cited of these.

I am of course indebted to Sandra Gilbert and Susan Gubar's ambitious feminist revision of Bloom's theory of influence in their first major collaborative effort, *The Madwoman in the Attic* (1979). Although Gilbert and Gubar have since revised their revision of Bloom for the modern period,[29] much that these critics have to say in their groundbreaking study of "the woman writer and the nineteenth-century literary imagination," which rightly stresses the importance of viewing literary production in some psychological and historical context, is true of the twentieth-century writing I have considered here as well. My discussion of Moore and Bishop clearly assumes as fact, for example, Gilbert and Gubar's suggestion that women writing in response to male-dominated traditions have composed work both "revisionary and revolutionary,"[30] and their observation that female authors have often "managed the difficult task of achieving true female literary authority by simultaneously conforming to and subverting patriarchal literary standards."[31]

However, substituting for Bloom's "anxiety of influence" their "anxiety of authorship," Gilbert and Gubar give us a strongly oppositional account of a "distinctly female literary tradition"[32]—a portrait of the literary battle of the sexes:

We must begin by redefining Bloom's seminal definitions of the revisionary "anxiety of influence." In doing so we will have to trace the difficult paths by which nineteenth-century women overcame their "anxiety of authorship," repudiated debilitating patriarchal prescriptions, and recovered or remembered the lost foremothers who could help them find their distinctive female power.[33]

Male-authored literature *in toto* is here depicted as a manifestation of oppressive patriarchal culture. The woman writer experiences the subjects and strategies, not to mention the sheer bulk, of writing by the opposite sex as inhibiting rather than enabling, and consequently must turn for example and a sense of empowerment to her "lost foremothers."

This version is canny, consolidating as it does the notion (adapted from Harold Bloom's antithetical criticism) that a distinctly female tradition has been formed in opposition to "patriarchal prescriptions," with that other notion (advanced by, for example, Adrienne Rich and Ellen Moers)[34] that a female tradition has been created by a more or less autonomous subculture of women writers who have learned from and extended the projects of their literary "foremothers." Yet Gilbert and Gubar's characterization of female writers' self-enabling activity pits "us" against "them" in a manner insufficiently attuned to the countless complicated and unpredictable ways in which real writers of either gender make use of their literary inheritance, through conscious or unconscious robbery and adaptation. A writer, as I have suggested, will gravitate toward different models, and toward different readings of or *versions* of those models, at different times in his or her life—for reasons having to do not only with gender but also with personal development and literary/historical moment. Both Moore and Bishop, as we have seen, find ways to debunk the potentially debilitating Romantic myth of imaginatively feminized nature, while Moore's relation to Browne and Bishop's relation to Herbert obviously show us a different, less intensely agonistic, portrait of male influence. One problem, then, with adopting *Madwoman* as a critical model is its generalizing stance, its failure sufficiently to distinguish one strand—or one response to one strand—of the male-authored tradition from another.

Similarly, Gilbert and Gubar's emphasis on "women's experience" in literature, while it opens up nineteenth-century fiction in a new way, also opens up a Pandora's box of problems for me as well as for other critics.[35] In their Preface the authors explain: "We have sought to describe both the experience that generates metaphor and the metaphor that creates experience. . . . Reading metaphors in this experiential way we have inevitably ended up reading our own lives as well as the texts we study."[36] On the one hand, reading writing by women in this experiential fashion can be culturally eye-opening and personally engaging. On the other hand, the authors' sense of what they call a "dis-eased" woman's tradition that records "central female experiences from a specifically female perspective"[37] against a background of patriarchal prescriptiveness leads to a notably limited description of female experience—emphasizing agoraphobia, claustrophobia, anorexia, bulimia, aphasia, and amnesia. Obviously, such a description fits some works better than others. *Madwoman* seems to me more elucidating, for instance, when it takes on Charlotte Bronte's *Jane Eyre* (a novel in the shape of an autobiography, clearly obsessed with social inequalities, female power, madness, and entrapment) than in its discussion of Emily Dickinson's permanently strange and mercurial metaphysical lyrics, which finally defy description in terms of "central female experiences." In the modern period, their theory fits the painfully confined and thrashing, aggressively confessional poetry of Sylvia Plath (to which the authors allude in their mention of sweeping imagistic and thematic patterns of coherence) far better than it fits the poetry of Moore or Bishop.

Further, this emphasis on female patterns of suffering

and struggle tends to highlight commonality while overlooking psychological and artistic difference. (Here one
might recall Elizabeth Bishop's objection, cited earlier, to
focussing on gender in art.) "The question which such an
assumption of the primacy of female experience in wom-
en's poems avoids asking is," as Jan Montefiore notes in
*Feminism and Poetry: Language, Experience, Identity in Wom-
en's Writing* (1987), "What makes a poem different from
autobiography, fictionalized or otherwise?"[38] And, I would
add, such an assumption often avoids probing other crucial
questions: How, and especially why, is one woman's poem
formally different from another's? What singular complex
of literary reactions and revisions has helped to make her
writing what it is?

If in Adrienne Rich's bold and much-cited 1971 essay
"When We Dead Awaken: Writing as Re-Vision," we find
a partial and highly personal answer to the last of these
questions, we also find the literary critical assumption of
what Montefiore calls the "primacy of experience," cou-
pled with the presupposition that male influence is generally debilitating. Rich's answer in this early piece to
"patriarchy—the domination of males" is a famous one, to
which I, like other feminist critics, am clearly indebted:
"Re-vision—the act of looking back, of seeing with fresh
eyes, of entering an old text from a new direction."[39]
Looking back at her own poetic beginnings in the conservative nineteen-fifties, Rich here associates male literary
influence with her early adoption of self-defeating de-
personalizing strategies, a confining "formalism" and an
"objective, observant tone." Development of her own writing, she claims, resulted partly from her reading of "older
women poets with their peculiar keenness and ambivalence: Sappho, Christina Rossetti, Emily Dickinson, Eli-
nor Wylie, Edna Millay, H.D." Marianne Moore, who
surely possessed, if anyone did, a "peculiar keenness and
ambivalence," is notably not included in this list, and is
mentioned only in passing as "the woman poet most

admired at the time (by men)."[40] Most importantly to Rich, her own writing has gained power from a growing courage, as she says, to write "directly about experiencing myself as a woman."[41] Discarding the "asbestos gloves" of formalism and writing in the first person "to and of women . . . out of a newly released courage to name, to love each other, to share risk and grief and celebration" emerges as the new ideal.[42] As Rich's testimony of her personal political and literary history, this early essay is admirably honest and urgent; many have found it inspiring. As a blueprint, though, for a new "woman's poetry"—and some feminists have read it as such—it can be both confusing (since we may wonder, given the variousness of individual female experience, what precisely it may mean to write "about experiencing myself as a woman"), and in its own way confining, a new "matriarchal prescriptiveness" replacing the old "patriarchal prescriptiveness."

Rich of course knows that to be a writer is to require not confinement but rather "a certain freedom of the mind":

> . . . freedom to press on, to enter the currents of your thought like a glider pilot, knowing that your motion can be sustained, that the buoyancy of your attention will not be suddenly snatched away. Moreover, if the imagination is to transcend and transform experience it has to question, to challenge, to conceive of alternatives, perhaps to the very life you are living at the moment. You have to be free to play around with the notion that day might be night, love might be hate; nothing can be too sacred for the imagination to turn into its opposite or to call experimentally by another name.[43]

And this eloquent acknowledgment of the artist's need for wholesale imaginative freedom leads Rich in turn to the following radical assertion, which both Moore and Bishop (neither of whom married and had children) also seem to have accepted as true, at least for their own lives: "to be a female human being trying to fulfill traditional female functions in a traditional way *is* in direct conflict with the subversive function of the imagination."[44] (In a later essay, Rich explains how she in fact came to value Bishop's poetry as expressive of "the essential outsiderhood of lesbian identity.")[45] That the same "subversive function" is at odds with *any* programmatic prescription of formal practices should be self-evident—including the prescription of evidently obligatory free verse, of the first-person pronoun, of delimited audience ("to women"), or of subject matter ("of women"). Poetic invention, as Marianne Moore observed more than sixty years ago, is necessarily at odds with the "Steam Roller" mentality that would "crush all particles down into close conformity."

A nonprogrammatic, "inductive" methodology as well as catholicity of taste is disarmingly proclaimed by Alicia Ostriker in the most ambitious recent feminist study of American women's poetry, *Stealing the Language: The Emergence of Women's Poetry in America* (1986):

> I attempt to read by the light that poems themselves emit, rather than by the fixed beam of one or another theory which might shine where a poem is not and leave in darkness the place were it is . . . my taste is eclectic. I admire closed and open forms, the pungency of colloquial idiom and the play of literary puns and allusions; evocative metaphor and clean abstraction; the disparate voices of lyric cry, satiric jibe, conversational inflection, prophetic incantation.[46]

But *Stealing the Language* does single out for attention and admiration a particular kind of poetry written by women in the last quarter century. This kind of poetry most often takes as its subjects the female body, female anger and violence, female eroticism and the desire for intimacy. It is writing that adopts as a conscious strategy what Ostriker (echoing Rich) calls "revisionist mythmaking," and that aggressively engages the reader's attention, tends toward colloquial, even purposefully crude, diction and as a rule employs the autobiographical "I." We are led to conclude, then, by this book—in which the most cited of a multitude of poets are Plath, Sexton, and Rich—that the most exciting and valuable writing by women in this country is a kind of neo-confessional poetry, "where," as the author puts it "women write strongly as women."[47]

Although Ostriker employs an eclectic methodology and discusses a wide array of female writers, "the lamp" of critical predisposition after all does (to advert to Wallace Stevens's "The Emperor of Ice-Cream") "affix its beam." Her focus naturally determines to some extent *whom* she includes in her story of "the emergence of women's poetry in America." (Marjorie Perloff has complained, for instance, that some writers thought of as avant-garde or "difficult," such as Susan Howe and Lorine Niedecker, are not included, not invited to Ostriker's "party.")[48] The focus also determines to some extent *what* Ostriker detects in individual poems, and more than a few times this "beam" may be said to "shine where a poem is not and leave in darkness the place where it is." Not surprisingly—given my own focus and predilections—the readings with which I most take issue are of some poems by Elizabeth Bishop.

In "Roosters," a two-part poem written during the Second World War and included in Bishop's 1946 collection *North & South*, Ostriker sees "a capsule representation of the invisible constraints inhibiting poets who would be ladies." She writes approvingly of the first part, in which Bishop serio-comically describes the stupidity and violence of burlesquely virile roosters, finding in it "a strong and brilliant parody of male brutality and male aesthetics." And she points to the following two tercets (particularly imbued with *un*ladylike bawdy innuendo) with particular approval:

> The crown of red
> set on your little head
> is charged with all your fighting blood.

> Yes, that excrescence
> makes a most virile presence,
> plus all that vulgar beauty of iridescence.

But the second section of the poem, which for the most part meditates on the rooster as a reminder of "St. Peter's sin" and as an emblem of forgiveness, she finds disappointingly timid and lacking in vitality:

> Imagery of the physical violence of cocks is thus succeeded not only by Christian moralizing on forgiveness but by a static use of the icon—brute life replaced by sacred (and forgiving) art—and by what is, after all, the cliché of the dawn. "Roosters" is finally a withdrawal of the familiar sort, its two parts rather crudely tacked together, ultimately detaching itself from what Pound called "an old bitch gone in the teeth, a botched civilization."[49]

(One might note in passing the irony that Ostriker here is quoting, presumably to remind us of a political engagement and boldness that she feels Bishop's poem ultimately lacks, a figure who, during the very war out of which Bishop writes, tragically acted out his own perverse and preposterous role as "a most virile presence.")

Two notions of "progress" it seems to me are implicated in Ostriker's reading of "Roosters." First is the premise, basal to *Stealing the Language*, that a separate tradition of women's poetry in America has progressed through stages of increasing female self-realization and freedom from male cultural and literary domination: from a circumscribed, genteel, and self-effacing poetry in the nineteenth century; to an early twentieth-century poetry (practiced by Sara Teasdale, Edna Millay, Louise Bogan, and others) written "personally from the heart"; to early modernist poetry (associated with Amy Lowell, Gertrude Stein, Mina Loy, H.D., and Marianne Moore) written "impersonally from the mind";[50] finally to its current culmination in the kind of neo-confessional poetry particularly admired by Ostriker, which often features physicality and anger, and which I have described above. Given this scheme, it is not hard to see why for Ostriker the second half of "Roosters" would have to be read as a loss of ground.

Of course, any description of progressive "emergence"

has emotional appeal: what literary woman is not for push-
ing back patriarchally induced constraints on women's
writing and speech? Who among us does not want to
believe the slogan, "You've come a long way?" And the
broad outline of developing poetic styles that Ostriker
proposes in her book is not unfamiliar. However, this
thinking leads on to the assumption that we are *now* in a
position to act as arbiters, deciding which experiences or
emotions are most honest or "authentic" (in this case anger
as more authentic than forgiveness). It suggests too, and
speciously, that when we come to evaluate the literary as
well as the social significance of a contemporary female
poet, what matters most is her "divestment of masks" in
work that is "impolite, crude, indecorous."[51] Somehow,
the headiness is all.

The second notion of progress inherent in Ostriker's
reading of "Roosters" is less global, more local—the suppo-
sition, which I have so far left unchallenged, that in this
particular poem as the speaker shifts the burden of her
attention from one rooster (the living creature, labeled as
"very combative" by the Greeks) to another (the Christian
emblem), she also clearly shifts allegiance from one emotion (anger) to another (forgiveness) and from one frame of
reference (brute life) to another (sacred art). A case has
been made, however, and meticulously supported, that
Bishop's poem embodies not this diachronic transformation so much as a kind of dialectic oscillation: " 'Roosters'
does not end, as Ostriker suggests, with a pietistic affirma-
tion of Christian orthodoxy, a neat turning of the other
cheek. The poem concludes, reduplicating its original dialectical dynamic in miniature, with a choice of similes,
neither of which holds privileged status."[52]

This reading by Susan Schweik I find more consistent
with Bishop's work as a whole. "Roosters," like others of
her poems—"Rain Towards Morning," "Love Lies Sleeping," "Sunday, 4 A.M.," "Insomnia," or the newly dis-
covered poem that begins "It is marvelous to wake up

together"[53]—engages in a kind of inconclusive musing associated with the liminal state between waking and sleeping,
when the drifting, associative mind takes up and mulls over
a set of problems or emotions, often indefinitely or mysteri-
ously linked to romantic love.[54] The mental excursus becomes embodied in chance images (here, roosters and the
sunrise) encountered by the speaker's almost hypnotically
engaged senses. At the moment, then, in "Roosters" when
Bishop describes the dawn as "the day's preamble/like wan-
dering lines in marble," we might see her as providing an
objective correlative for her own just-awake, freely associative or meandering thought process. Surely, the final tercet
of the poem is in keeping with Bishop's recurrent musing
pattern—and more consonant with Schweik's "dialectical"
reading than with Ostriker's charge of pietistic retreat:

> The sun climbs in,
> following "to see the end,"
> faithful as enemy, or friend.

Characteristically inconclusive, wary of anthropocentric
metaphor, and wry, this ending is neither appeasingly
"sunny" nor stale—not, as Ostriker charges, a "cliché of
the dawn."

Ostriker writes more favorably of Bishop's later poem,
"The Moose," which she finds more conformable to the
new "women's poetry" in its reversal of "the assumption of
man's division from nature."[55] Contrasting "The Moose"
with Robert Frost's "The Most of It," Ostriker finds in the
latter poem an example of male separation from nature, in
the former an example of female synthesis. Explicating that
moment in Bishop's poem when the bus passengers (and by
extension, Bishop's readers) are transfixed by their sudden
encounter with a female moose on the road, Ostriker pre-
sumes to answer the poet's question:

> Why, why do we feel
> (we all feel) this sweet
> sensation of joy?

"Why do we feel this joy? The answer can only be that we have recognized in nature, ourselves."[56] But like so many images in Bishop's poems, the moose is (to borrow Helen Vendler's terms) both "domestic" and "strange"; separated from the passengers by the humanly fashioned shell of the bus and then by the acrid smell of gasoline, the creature is at once "homely" and "otherworldly." It is more likely that the moose (or nature) possesses transfixing and trans- forming power precisely because we recognize in it *not* merely ourselves, but rather the reassuring presence of some irrefutable "other."

Following Vendler's earlier example,[57] Ostriker pairs Bishop's poem with Frost's and offers some shrewd specific observations (e.g., that the word "look" is here repeated three times, "as if completing the triplet utterance of fairy tale or ritual").[58] What I take issue with here and throughout is a tendency finally to simplify along "if they, then we" lines. If men are warlike and "cocky" like roosters, then we women are innocent victims, whose most appropriate re- sponse is righteous anger. (But "Roosters," in fact, more complexly suggests that those "rustling wives" who "ad- mire" the roosters' pompous posturing and who lead "hens' lives/of being courted and despised," are themselves com- plicit in the violent order.) If men are, as far as nature is concerned, incommunicado, then women are in commu- nion. (In fact, both Frost's "The Most of It," in which the "embodiment" of nature appears as a buck or a "he," and Bishop's "The Moose," in which the symbolic creature is a "she," resist these reductive characterizations.) And, as per- haps the most strikingly partisan example of if/then formu- lation: "If the deep truth discoverable in men's poems is that all men are each other's rivals, the equal and opposite truth discoverable in women's poems is that we are allies and portions of one another."[59]

Insisting upon "equal and opposite" terms, Ostriker simply adopts a counter–Bloomian mythic model for liter- ary influence:

I use the Bloomian term ["strong mothers"] not because I believe that the woman poet's achievement depends on killing and superseding her predecessor. Rather than Oedipus and Laius at the crossroads, the model among women writers, critics as well as poets, is Demeter and Kore: except that it is the daughter who descends to Hades, step by step, to retrieve and revive a mother who has been raped, or perhaps seduced, by a powerful male god.[60]

The schematic black and white pairings that we find here—rivals versus allies, killing versus reviving, rapist versus victim—are, interestingly enough, proposed by a female poet and critic who begins her book by acknowledging her own indebtedness not to a literary foremother but to William Blake, thus reminding us of what is a far more intricate intertextual and intersexual literary reality.[61]

Finally, Sandra Gilbert and Susan Gubar assay a more elaborate account of literary influence in *The War of the Words* (1987), the first volume of *No Man's Land*, their three-volume study of the modern period. Indeed, with the "female affiliation complex,"[62] their latest feminist revision of Bloom's theory, the authors posit a paradigm almost as labyrinthine and qualified as their larger argument about the modernist battle of the sexes is simple and sweeping.

Gilbert and Gubar cite Freud's account in "Female Sexuality" of the three paths open to a young girl entering the oedipal phase, and then translate that account into a three-branched model of female literary options: either a "feminine" submission to powerful paternal precursors, or a kind of aesthetic frigidity or relinquishing of literary desire, or a claiming of female precursors associated with recalcitrant preoedipalism and the Freudian "masculinity complex." But their adoption of this psychosexual model immediately provokes demurrals within their own work. They protest, for instance, that they do not accept Freud's valuation of sexual options, in which the normative path is the adoption of the father as love object; they grant that they are not dealing with inexorable biological lineage, as is Freud, but rather with the voluntary establishment of quasi-familial literary continua; they acknowledge that the "literary implications of female autonomy," which they then discuss at some length, fall entirely outside the parameters of the psychoanalytic paradigm. Gilbert and Gubar's model does make room, as Ostriker's mythic model does not, for a range of reactions to literary parentage, including the ambivalent response of modern female authors to a newly expanded and formidable inheritance of women's writing. But if Ostriker's theorizing tends toward the black and white, Gilbert and Gubar's adaptation of Freudian theory is gray—murky in its strained and qualified analogizing, and predictable in its emphasis (following *The Madwoman*) on twentieth-century sexual anxieties and antagonisms.

Commitment to the notion of literary modernism as both record and result of a struggle between the sexes leads Gilbert and Gubar to sort through the writing they discuss, picking out kernels to add to their "conflict" pile and ignoring the rest as chaff. They sometimes interpret parts of works out of context. A small example is their suggestion that the phrase "dynasties of negative constructions/ darkening and dying" in Bishop's "Invitation to Miss Marianne Moore" refers to oppressive dynasties of male literary construction, which overlooks the more plausible explanation that Bishop is playfully poking fun at her older friend's notorious use of double negatives and litotes.[63] The argument of *The War* generally avoids taking into account other issues involved in the birth of modernism: class struggle, for instance, or heightened self-consciousness about the opposition between abstraction and experience, or the literary reaction against nineteenth-century mannerism. And it omits related discussion of what male and female authors might have in common.

Embedded as it is in a simple "metastory, a story of stories about gender strife,"[64] Gilbert and Gubar's "female affiliation complex," which takes psychosexual analogizing about as far as it can go, nevertheless does begin to suggest the almost daedal complexities of literary relationship. "We inevitably find," the authors allow, "women writers oscillating between their matrilineage and patrilineage in an arduous process of self-definition."[65] The work of Moore and Bishop (and others, to be sure) suggests that within the poet's mind and work this "oscillation" may be so rapid as effectively to blur distinction.

Of course, Moore's and Bishop's personal and literary interactions *do* in some ways fit popular conceptions of matrilineage and patrilineage. For instance, Marianne and Mrs. Moore (who in private correspondence referred to themselves as "Rat" and "Mole," respectively) may be said to have established their own idiosyncratic "autonomous female tradition." In a 1941 letter to her close friend Hildegarde Watson, Moore acknowledges Mrs. Moore's silent collaboration and links her own penchant for literary pack-ratting in general back to her mother, who provided her with so many phrases and ideas for poems: " 'Satisfaction is a lowly thing how pure a thing is joy.' (I got the idea from Mole.) Am worse than a rodent about appropriating,—as you know."[66]

Moore and Bishop's mentor/protégée relationship would also seem to support the notion of a self-fertilizing female tradition. And the fact that Bishop not only solicited Moore's advice in the early years of their correspondence but also gently resisted Moore's formidable moral and maternal sway reinforces Gilbert and Gubar's argument in *The War of the Words* that this female inheritance is newly fraught with ambivalence for the twentieth-century woman writer. Certainly, these poets' lifelong friendship as well as their separate establishment of households exclusively with other women—Moore with her mother, and Bishop, most lastingly, with her Brazilian companion Lota de Macedo Soares—sustains the observation, frequently made by feminist critics, that female support networks are crucial for creative women, whose work has generally not flourished under the heterosexual and familial dispensations of our culture. In their extensive correspondence, Moore and Bishop show concern for one another's health and finances, bolster one another's egos, and express respectfully restrained but unqualified affection for each other—all of which may have been more crucial to their ongoing productivity than any specifically critical exchange.[67] And finally, as my chapters on these poets' responses to Romanticism point out, both Moore and Bishop came up with strategies that lend credence to the idea (espoused by almost all feminist theorists) that women writers, with varying degrees of subtlety or strenuousness, re-see and revise what Gertrude Stein called "patriarchal poetry."

But what becomes of our concepts of linearity (either matri- or patri-) when we consider that both Moore's and Bishop's seventeenth-century male models are so powerfully associated with female figures—Sir Thomas Browne with Mrs. Moore's religiosity and grammatical scrupulousness, George Herbert with Marianne Moore as well as with Bishop's lost Nova Scotian world of mother and home? Study of these particular women poets forces us to acknowledge more than the insidious biases and possible deleterious effects of the "patriarchal tradition," and more than the encouraging (or simultaneously encouraging and discouraging) example of a "matriarchal tradition." Rather, it points to a more perplexing mingling in the imagination—to a kind of maternal transformation and assimilation of congenial male sources.

And in this particular imaginative mixture, brew, or writing "solution," literary experience is of course combined with peculiar biographical fact. Both Moore and Bishop experienced their biological fathers only as absences. One might speculate that as a result they were anxious to locate literary "fathers," but at the same time less likely than female poets who were actually subject to domineering fathers (such as Emily Dickinson) to replay the family scenario by struggling in their poetry with powerful, simultaneously desirable and oppressive masculine precursors.[68] Both Moore and Bishop chose late Renaissance male models who were connected to issues, impressed in their early childhoods, of sanity and religion; who demonstrated a sense of Protestant humility that, as Bonnie Costello has suggested, in some ways resembles culturally approved, traditional feminine humility;[69] who were rather "minor," or peripheral to the central canon of Anglo-American literature; and who—partly because they were somewhat peripheral, partly because they were not associated with popular Renaissance themes of sexual assault and seduction—may have seemed to each modern poet more unthreatening, more like herself, and more amenable than others of his contemporaries to imaginative "shaping" and assimilation into her largely woman-centered world.

How does a gifted woman enable her own writing in a male-predominant culture and in response to what is still a male-preponderant literary canon? What both Moore and Bishop consistently rejected or resisted were those elements of male-authored literature that would tend to silence them—each freely borrowing or reassembling whatever seemed to her (at her moment in literary history and given her own personal obsessions) useful or enabling. Strongly oppositional feminist theories of literary influence—which developed out of a concern for the fate of women in our culture and for the fate of the productions of cultured women—have tended to overlook such positive intersections and interactions. It is evident that what we now need are more flexible approaches to reading that, while firmly committed to the same feminist concerns, acknowledge and allow more for discussion of the layered complexities—as folded and refolded as an Appalachian geosyncline—that characterize the finest women poets' (and all our most accomplished poets') individual relations to their literary inheritance. The poetic imagination, after all, has many methods of survival, and the uses of tradition remain inexhaustible and unpredictable.

It is true that neither Marianne Moore nor Elizabeth Bishop proffered extended literary theories. Neither, in an age of polemic, engaged in polemics. Both poets did, however, leave bodies of work that can be read as challenges to the limitations of current critical constructs, since they encourage less narrowly programmatic, yet authentically feminist, ways of viewing and re-viewing literature and the world. It is time to reverse the earlier guilty verdict of some feminist critics. Neither Moore nor Bishop wrote, as some feminist writers have implied, to please men.[70] Rather, they wrote as poets—who cannot, after all, be narrowly confined to the role of sociologist or political advocate—must write:

> Openly, yes.
> with the naturalness
>   of the hippopotamus or the alligator
>   when it climbs out on the bank to experience the
>
> sun, I do these
> things which I do, which please
>   no one but myself.[71]

A few more observations may illustrate how both Moore and Bishop undercut male pomposity and imperiousness, deploring the fact (as Moore put it in "Marriage") "that men have power/and sometimes one is made to feel it." That power may be in the form of a boorish "man looking into the sea," or of "monopolists/of 'stars, garters, buttons/and other shining baubles' " ("Marriage"); in the form of preening, combative roosters, or of rapacious sixteenth-century conquistadors, tramping through the South American jungle (and stalking native women) to the tune of "*L'Homme armé*" ("Brazil, January 1, 1502"). Everywhere, their poetry implicitly supports the moral assertion that under no conditions is a woman's identity or fate to be considered less significant than that of a man. (As just a few obvious examples, see Moore's "Sojourn in the Whale" or "Paper Nautilus," Bishop's "Filling Station" or "In the Waiting Room.") Whether through satiric jabs or subtle subversions of androcentric tropes, through serious development of subjects that have generally not been treated seriously by male poets, or simply through purposeful attention to their own metaphysical dilemmas and observations, these poets repeatedly cause us to recognize that a woman's spiritual experience is every bit as much "at the center," and as representative, as a man's.

But only *as much* at the center. If, as I would argue, both Moore and Bishop overturn the long-standing cultural assumption that males somehow exist at the center of reality and females at the periphery, they do not then assert a "gynocentricity" equal and opposite to male "phallocentricity." What I think particularly large and important about these women poets, besides their extraordinary talent, is their thoroughgoing (if sometimes subtle) resistance to *all forms* of egocentricity and domination. Rather than relying on the central, self-exposed and often self-congratulatory "I," they make room for multiple and juxtaposed perspectives—both human and nonhuman—reminding us that no matter what position we occupy there is always, as Emily Dickinson asserted, "Another — way to see."

Consider, for example, the way that Marianne Moore (who was "not," in her own words, "matrimonially ambitious") credits views and accommodates voices other than her own through her habit of frequent quotation—as here, in her evocation of a hypothetical Adam's experience of sexual desire and of the institution of "Marriage":

Unnerved by the nightingale
and dazzled by the apple,
impelled by "the illusion of a fire
effectual to extinguish fire,"

compared with which
the shining of the earth
is but deformity—a fire
"as high as deep
as bright as broad
as long as life itself,"
he stumbles over marriage,
"a very trivial object indeed"
to have destroyed the attitude
in which he stood—
the ease of the philosopher
unfathered by a woman.

Or consider the way that Moore's poems often remain delicately poised between two contradictory points of view. We see, for example, in the sea-scrubbed New England coastal town of "The Steeple-Jack" an ambiguous Eden—at once pristine and slightly sinister; in the elaborate Louis Fifteenth candelabrum of "No Swan So Fine" an example of the double-edged victory and vainglory of artifice; in the historically rich and naturally lush state of Virginia ("Virginia Britannia") evidence at once of breathtaking democratic diversity and deplorable imperialist arrogance.

Then too, there is the wholly original brand of literary criticism that Moore invented during her years at *The Dial*, which allowed her an elaborately orchestrated interplay of viewpoints. Here, for example, in her 1921 review of Eliot's collection of critical essays, *The Sacred Wood*, she manages to resist Eliot's programmatic modernist dismissal of Swinburne; then to praise Eliot (using his own words) for possessing an intensity and a seriousness of purpose that Swinburne lacks; and, finally, to applaud Eliot for his dedication to the living tradition—but here citing Swinburne again, so that her final praise yet contains a sort of subtle reprise of her earlier gentle correction. The effect of the whole glints with wit and is nimble, or, as Moore says of Eliot's poetry, "troutlike":

There is about Swinburne the atmosphere of magnificence, a kind of permanent association of him with King Solomon 'perfumed with all the powders of the merchants, approaching in his litter'—an atmosphere which is not destroyed, one feels, even by indiscriminate browsing. . .Although Swinburne was not as Mr. Eliot says he was not, 'tormented by the restless desire to penetrate to the heart and marrow of a poet,' it is apparent that Mr. Eliot is. In his poetry, he seems to move troutlike through a multiplicity of foreign objects and in his instinctiveness and care as a critic, he appears as a complement to the sheen upon his poetry. In his opening a door upon the past and indicating what is there, he recalls the comment made by Swinburne upon Hugo:

> Art knows nothing of death; . . . all that ever had life in it, has life in it forever; those themes only are dead which never were other than dead. No form is obsolete, no subject out of date, if the right man be there to rehandle it.[72] [CPrMM, pp. 53–55]

Here, as elsewhere in her *Dial* criticism, Moore challenges the doctrinaire or monophonic in modernism, inventing through an intermingling of voices her unique, almost choral criticism. We might even say that Moore's exact and exacting *Dial* commentaries, taken cumulatively, constitute a sort of polemic-against-polemic. It is not that she holds no strong aesthetic values and opinions. And she is certainly capable, as this assessment of the 1936 literary scene proves, of the tart and pithy: "Judged by our experimental writing, we are suffering today from unchastity, sadism, blasphemy, and rainsoaked foppishness" (CPrMM, p. 344). But in her criticism as in her poetry, Moore's approach is insistently polyvocal. There is always, she is always reminding us with her radical ambiguities and her clustered quotations, with what she called her "hybrid method of composition," more than one way of seeing or speaking about any one thing.

Like Moore, Bishop finds ways to evade the circumscribed and the dogmatic by entertaining contradictory viewpoints simultaneously. Her poems are peppered with brief, simply phrased but intellectually and emotionally complex indecisions: "enemy, or friend"; "commerce or contemplation"; "*Mont d'Espoir* or *Mount Despair*"; "awful but cheerful." On a larger scale, "Crusoe in England" ambiguously expresses both social and antisocial impulses, both antagonism toward and nostalgia for Crusoe's enforced island solitude; and the two-part "Roosters," as we have seen, oscillates between two views of roosters and between two different cultural perspectives.

Elizabeth Bishop's poetry (in this way in the tradition of Donne and Herbert) is more dramatic than Moore's, and she relies not so much on quotation to create a multiplicity of voices as on the actual creation of situation and character. This dramatic preference is manifest in her short stories— such as "Gwendolyn," "Memories of Uncle Neddy," or "In the Village," which reproduce characters and voices from Bishop's Nova Scotian childhood. And in poems such as "The Man-Moth," "The Prodigal," "The Gentleman of Shalott" or "Crusoe in England," Bishop invents or adapts dramatis personae who provide at once an opportunity for discretely disguised autobiography and for the evocation of various alien or auslander positions. With the adoption of these personae (as with her adoption of George Herbert as a literary model) Bishop shows her affinity for the perplexed and in one way or another "peripheral" male figure.

In general for Bishop, the "minor female Wordsworth," it is the minority, the culturally "marginal" or disenfranchised point of view that is especially worth preserving: the bluesy pragmatist's, for example, in "Songs for a Colored Singer" (for Billie Holiday): "I'm going to go and take the bus/and find someone monogamous." Or the doomed Brazilian burglar and murderer's in "The Burglar of Babylon":

"Ninety years they gave me.
　　Who wants to live that long?
I'll settle for ninety hours,
　　On the hill of Babylon.

Or the view of an actual "minor"—the turn-of-the-century Brazilian schoolgirl, preserved in Bishop's translation from the Portuguese of *The Diary of 'Helena Morley'*: "I'm almost fourteen years old and already I think more than all the rest of the family. I think I began to draw conclusions from the age of ten years, or less. And I swear I never saw anybody from mama's family think about things. They hear something and believe it; and that's that for the rest of their lives. They're all happy like that!"[73]

It might be argued that Moore's and Bishop's insistence on juxtaposing human perspectives and presenting a variety of voices is neither particularly unusual, nor especially related to gender. Their poetry, after all, comes out of an age of self-conscious perspectivism: we see it in Faulkner's fiction; in cubist paintings; in the personae of Yeats and Pound. What is, I am suggesting, especially fresh and striking—aside from each writer's invention of unique ways to admit the polyphonic and polysemous—is the continuous and unbroken link in these poets' work (not to be found in the work of Pound, Lowell, and others) between multiple perspectivism and a strong distaste for dogmatism, egocentricity, and domination. I would not claim that male writers have never, or never will in the future, take similar stands—but rather that in the cases of these two female writers disaffection is rooted in the experience of women who have themselves been "made to feel" the power of others.

The determination to eschew all forms of imperiousness and imperialism shapes not only Moore's and Bishop's attitude toward other human beings, but their poetic approach to the nonhuman world as well. If nature and woman commonly have been identified with one another in our culture, and if men have on the whole assumed "natural" or God-given dominion over both, these women poets refuse that identification and resist that dominion. In their work nature (as embodied in creatures and other natural phenomena) remains clearly "other"—apart from men and women—with its own authority, and with its own separate perspective or "look": Moore's sea can also see, and is "quick to return a rapacious look"; Bishop's moose "looks the bus over." This unsentimental but respectful approach to nature seems to me an appropriately nonappropriative extension of feminism. It is a position that is not, I would add, in a time when so many forms of life are already no longer present to meet our gaze, politically negligible.

Although Moore is fascinated by the emblematic potential of nature, and although Bishop capitalizes on the possibilities nature affords for indirect self-expression, neither poet identifies with those other forms of life merely so as to speak through them, or for them, which would be sentimentality and perhaps something like fraud. A glacier, or pine trees with emerald turkey feet at the top, volcanoes, the isinglass irises of a fish: all such phenomena retain their essential nonhuman strangeness. As if hovering briefly at the border of human identity, these poets linger long enough to report back the reminder that the "other"—in the form of a paper nautilus, a pangolin, a cat with "alligator eyes," an armadillo, a moose, a rabbit "with fixed, ignited eyes"—exists. Exists independently, and as much at the center as any woman or man. If this is humility—and it is—it can also be, as their works make clear, an enabling artistic stance.

Notes

Abbreviations

CPrMM is used throughout the text to designate *The Complete Prose of Marianne Moore,* ed. Patricia C. Willis (New York: Viking, 1986).

CPrEB is used throughout the text to designate *Elizabeth Bishop: The Collected Prose,* ed. Robert Giroux (New York: Farrar, Straus & Giroux, 1984).

Introduction

1. T. S. Eliot, "The Function of Criticism," *Selected Essays* (New York: Harcourt, Brace & Co., 1950), p. 13.
2. Harold Bloom, in his Introduction to *American Women Poets* (New York: Chelsea House, 1986), p. 2.
3. I was fortunate to come into contact at Berkeley with Robert Pinsky, an early proponent of Bishop's, who saw her later work as addressing important poetic and philosophic issues— the relation of mind and world, self and other. See Pinsky's "The Idiom of a Self: Elizabeth Bishop and Wordsworth," *Elizabeth Bishop and Her Art,* eds. Lloyd Schwartz and Sybil P.

Estess (Ann Arbor: University of Michigan Press, 1983), pp. 49–60.

4. Suzanne Juhasz, *Naked and Fiery Forms: Modern American Poetry by Women* (New York: Harper & Row, 1976), p. 35. Some feminist critics have recently begun to consider the feminist re-vision and subversiveness of Moore's work. See, for some examples:

> Carolyn A. Durham, "Linguistic and Sexual Engendering in Marianne Moore's Poetry," *Engendering the Word*, ed. Temma F. Berg (Chicago: University of Illinois Press, 1989), pp. 224–243.
>
> Leigh Gilmore, "The Gaze of the Other Woman: Beholding and Begetting in Dickinson, Moore, and Rich," Berg, *Engendering the Word*, pp. 81–102.
>
> Vicki Graham, "Whetted to Brilliance," *Sagetrieb* 6, no. 3 (Winter 1987): pp. 127–146.
>
> Jeredith, Merrin "Re-Seeing the Sea: Marianne Moore's 'A Grave' as a Woman Writer's Re-Vision," *Marianne Moore: Woman and Poet* (Orono, Maine: National Poetry Foundation, 1990).
>
> Alicia Ostriker, "What Do Women (Poets) Want?: Marianne Moore and H.D. as Poetic Ancestresses," *Poesis* 6, no. 3 and 4 (double issue) (1985): pp. 1–9.
>
> Susan Schweik, "Writing War Poetry Like a Woman," *Critical Inquiry* 13, no. 3 (Spring 1987): pp. 532–556.

5. It is interesting that Moore and Bishop also praised one another in terms of "freshness." See, for example, Moore's letter to Bishop of 27 October 1954, in which she responds to her younger friend's praise of her *Fables of La Fontaine*: " . . . and that *you*, Elizabeth, whose speciality is freshness and flavor should call it fresh and transparent!"

Letters from Moore to Bishop are in Rare Books and Manuscripts, Vassar College Library, Poughkeepsie, N.Y., which is the source for all such letters referred to and excerpted in this text.

6. Letters from Bishop to Moore are in the Marianne Moore Collection, the Rosenbach Museum and Library, Philadelphia, which is the source for all such letters referred to and excerpted in this text. (Rosenbach V:04:30).

7. Bonnie Costello, "Marianne Moore and Elizabeth Bishop: Friendship and Influence," *Twentieth Century Literature* 30, nos. 2 and 3 (1984): p. 131. (Reprinted in *American Women Poets.*)

8. The Herbert poem to which Bishop refers is "Our Life is Hid with Christ in God." *The English Works of George Herbert*, vol. 2, ed. George Herbert Palmer (New York: Houghton Mifflin, 1905), p. 283. (Bishop's letter, Rosenbach V:05:02.)

9. For other discussions of the early years of Moore's and Bishop's relationship, see the following works:

    Costello's "Friendship and Influence" (cited earlier).
    Lynn Keller, "Words Worth a Thousand Postcards: The Bishop/ Moore Correspondence," *American Literature* 55 (1983): pp. 405–429.
    David Kalstone, "Trial Balances: Elizabeth Bishop and Marianne Moore," *Grand Street* 3 (Autumn 1983): pp. 115–135.

10. Lynn Keller in "Words Worth a Thousand Postcards" and Bonnie Costello in "Friendship and Influence" both discuss the "Roosters" exchange of 16 October 1940 (from Moore) and 17 October 1940 (Bishop's reply).

11. For an early example of Moore's bolstering of Bishop's artistic confidence, consider their August 1936 correspondence. Two years out of college, Bishop briefly falters in her sense of calling:

    I cannot, cannot decide what to do—I am even considering studying medicine or bio-chemistry, and have procured all sorts of catalogues, etc. I feel that I have given myself more than a fair trial, and the accomplishment has been nothing at all. [Rosenbach V:04:30]

    And Moore replies:

    What you say about studying medicine does not disturb me at all; for interesting as medicine is, I feel you would not be able to give up writing, with the ability for it that you have; but it does disturb me that you should have the *feeling* that it might be well to give it up. To have produced what you have—either verse or prose is enviable, and you certainly would not suppose that such method as goes with a precise and proportioning ear, is "contemporary" or usual. [Vassar College Library]

12. Bonnie Costello introduces these helpful terms in "Friendship and Influence," although she does not employ them, as I do here, in ways specifically related to Moore's and Bishop's uses of literary tradition.

13. Elizabeth Bishop, "Influences," *American Poetry Review* 14 (January/February 1985): p. 12. This is an edited transcript of a talk given on 13 December 1977, for the Academy of American Poets. Moore herself cites this Herbert poem as an example of successful concentration in her essay "Humility, Concentration, and Gusto."

14. Bishop quotes the phrase from a college theme by M. W. Croll entitled "Gerard Manley Hopkins: Notes on Timing in his Poetry." See M. W. Croll, "The Baroque Style in Prose," *Studies in English Philology* (Minneapolis: University of Minnesota, 1929). In an interview, the mature Bishop expressed the same idea, saying that she admired Hopkins's attempt "to dramatize the mind in action rather than repose." See Ashley Brown, "An Interview with Elizabeth Bishop," *Elizabeth Bishop and Her Art*, eds. Lloyd Schwartz and Sybil P. Estess (Ann Arbor: University of Michigan Press, 1983), p. 298. In his recent book, *Elizabeth Bishop: Her Artistic Development* (Charlottesville: University Press of Virginia, 1988), Thomas J. Travisano discusses Bishop's theory of poetry with reference to these remarks about Baroque prose and Hopkins. See especially the section of his book entitled "The Mind in Action," pp. 63–73.

15. The phrase from Herbert's poem appears, long after her "imitation," "The Weed," was composed, in Bishop's letter of 8 January 1964 to Anne Stevenson: "My outlook is pessimistic. I think we are still barbarians. . . . But I think we should be gay in spite of it, sometimes even giddy, to make life endurable and to keep ourselves 'new, tender, quick.' " Cited by Costello in "Friendship and Influence," p. 148.

16. Lynn Keller employs these terms of contrast in her detailed discussion of Bishop's adaptation and postmodern modification of Moore's modernist poetic techniques in *Re-making It New* (New York: Cambridge University Press, 1987), Chapters 3 and 4.

17. Bishop to Moore, 31 January 1938. (Rosenbach V:05:01.)

18. Moore to Bishop, 29 January 1957. (Vassar College Library.)

19. See Ashley Brown, "An Interview with Elizabeth Bishop," Schwartz and Estess, *Elizabeth Bishop and Her Art,* p. 294.

20. See T. S. Eliot, *George Herbert.* British Council: Writers and Their Work, no. 152, 1962.

21. Marianne Moore cites Pound in her review of "The Cantos," *The Complete Prose of Marianne Moore,* ed. Patricia C. Willis (New York: Viking, 1986), p. 272. All subsequent references to this book appear in text abbreviated CPrMM.

22. Marianne Moore, "His Shield," *The Complete Poems of Marianne Moore* (New York: Macmillan/Viking, 1981), p. 144. (All subsequent excerpts of Moore's poems are from this text unless otherwise noted.) An earlier, published version of my Chapter 1 also made this connection. See " 'To Explain Grace Requires a Curious Hand': Marianne Moore and the Literary Tradition," *Poesis* 6, no. 1 (1984): pp. 16–39. Geoffrey Hartman notes the connection of armor with spiritual combat in Moore's poetry in "Six Women Poets," *Easy Pieces* (New York: Columbia University Press, 1985), p. 111: "Her recurrent images of Armor ('His Shield,' 'The Pangolin') are linked to the theme of Spiritual Combat and come ultimately from Paul's letter to the Ephesians; the armor she describes is the modesty whereby the self is made strong to resist itself, but also strong to assert its being against voracious dogmatisms."

23. Elizabeth Bishop, "The Bight," *The Complete Poems 1927–1979* (New York: Farrar, Straus & Giroux, 1983), p. 60. All subsequent excerpts of Bishop's poems are from this text unless otherwise noted.

24. Margaret Homans describes this traditional, and problematic, Romantic objectification of women in *Women Writers and Poetic Identity* (Princeton: Princeton University Press, 1980).

25. Ezra Pound, "A Retrospect," *Literary Essays,* ed. T. S. Eliot (New York: New Directions, 1968), p. 11.

26. See Carol T. Christ, *Victorian and Modern Poetics* (Chicago: University of Chicago Press, 1984). Christ demonstrates how "modernist poets explore ways of objectifying poetry that show striking continuities with Victorian poetics." However, the modernists themselves, for a number of reasons

that Christ also explores, insistently disavowed this continuity with their Victorian predecessors.

Chapter 1

1. Laurence Stapleton, *Marianne Moore: The Poet's Advance* (Princeton: Princeton University Press, 1978), p. 57.
2. The Papers of Marianne Moore, Rosenbach Museum and Library, Philadelphia. Moore's private reading lists for her freshman and sophomore years appear in the *Marianne Moore Newsletter*, ed. Patricia Willis, 5, no. 1, Spring 1981. (The *Newsletter* is now defunct.)
3. Glenway Wescott, "Concerning Miss Moore's Observations," *The Dial* 78 (1925): p. 4.
4. Louise Bogan, "American to Her Backbone," reprinted in *A Poet's Alphabet* (New York: McGraw-Hill, 1970), p. 307.
5. I use the term "objectivism" here as related to, but broader than, the "Objectivism" espoused by Louis Zukofsky in the 1920s. I mean by it the focus on concrete particulars that characterizes so much of the poetry we call "modern." For a similar use of the term in relation to Moore's poetics, see Chapter 1 of Bernard F. Engel's *Marianne Moore* (New York: Twayne, 1964), and Kenneth Burke's essay "Motives and Motifs in the Poetry of Marianne Moore" in *Marianne Moore: A Collection of Critical Essays*, ed. Charles Tomlinson (Englewood Cliffs, N.J.: Prentice-Hall, 1969).
6. Ezra Pound, *The Spirit of Romance* (New York: New Directions, 1968), p. 18. (Originally published by J. M. Dent in 1910.) Marianne Moore singled out *The Spirit of Romance* in her 1961 Paris Review interview with Donald Hall: "I don't think anybody could read that book and feel that a flounderer was writing." *A Marianne Moore Reader* (New York: Viking, 1961), p. 271.
7. Pound, "The Serious Artist," *Literary Essays* (New York: New Directions, 1968), p. 48.
8. Pound, "Marianne Moore and Mina Loy," reprinted in Tomlinson, *Marianne Moore,* pp. 46–47.
9. Bonnie Costello, *Marianne Moore: Imaginary Possessions* (Cambridge: Harvard University Press, 1981), p. 5.

10. The paper nautilus and the coral snake were gifts from Elizabeth Bishop, as Bishop recounts in her "Efforts of Affection," *Elizabeth Bishop: The Collected Prose*, ed. Robert Giroux (New York: Farrar, Straus & Giroux, 1984), pp. 134–135. The former was, as she says, a "very successful gift"; the latter was not.

11. Wallace Stevens, "Sunday Morning," *The Collected Poems* (New York: Knopf, 1975).

12. Steven Mullaney, "Strange Things, Gross Terms, Curious Customs: The Rehearsal of Cultures in the Late Renaissance," *Representations* 3 (Summer 1983): p. 40.

13. Edmund Gosse, *Sir Thomas Browne* (London: Macmillan, 1905), p. 162.

14. Edward Topsell, *The Historie of Foure-Footed Beastes* (London: William Jaggard, 1607). From University Microfilms, Inc., Ann Arbor, Michigan, reproduced from the copy in the Huntington Library. (A reproduction of the copy at the Bodleian Library, Oxford, is also available from Da Capo Press [New York, 1973].)

15. Scofield Thayer, "Comment," *The Dial* LXXVIII (1925): pp. 265–268.

16. Stapleton, *Marianne Moore*, p. 129.

17. *The Works of Sir Thomas Browne*, ed. Geoffrey Keynes (Chicago: University of Chicago Press, 1964), 4 vols., vol. 1: pp. 24–25. Subsequent references, with volume number designated, refer to this text.

18. Certainly there are passages in the *Religio* that a modern reader would find intolerant and anti-Semitic, but even in these passages Browne does not preach hatred: ". . . neither doth herein my zeal so farre make me forget the generall charitie I owe unto humanity, as rather to hate then pity Turkes, Infidels, and (what is worse) [the] Jews, rather contenting my selfe to enjoy that happy stile, then maligning those who refuse so glorious a title" (*Religio*, Part I, sec. 1). Browne did, as he attests in his *Religio*, believe in the existence of witches. I am not suggesting that Moore's own religious and spiritual beliefs precisely matched Browne's, but rather that she found in him a figure who stood in his own time—taking into account the greater religious restrictions and dangers of that time—for a spirit of religious toleration.

19. See Geoffrey Keynes's Introduction to *Sir Thomas Browne: Selected Writings* (London: Faber & Faber, 1968).
20. In her remarks on the acceptance of the National Book Award, Moore said, "I can see no reason for calling my work poetry except that there is no other category in which to put it" (CPrMM, p. 648).
21. Some of Moore's drawings appear as cover illustrations for the *Marianne Moore Newsletter*, published by the Rosenbach Museum and Library, Philadelphia.
22. Marianne Moore, *Poems* (London: Egoist Press, 1921).
23. Harold Bloom in his Editor's Note to *Modern Critical Views: Marianne Moore*, ed. Harold Bloom (New York: Chelsea House, 1987), p. vii.
24. Marie Borroff, *Language and the Poet: Verbal Artistry in Frost, Stevens, and Moore* (Chicago: University of Chicago Press, 1979).
25. For citation of authority in the form of quotation (a feature found both in Moore's poems and in advertising), Robert Burton's *Anatomy of Melancholy*, even more than the work of Browne, is the prime seventeenth-century example.
26. Borroff, *Language and the Poet,* p. 126.
27. Ibid, p. 80.
28. Ibid, p. 110.
29. See T. S. Eliot's Introduction to Moore's *Selected Poems* (New York: Macmillan, 1935).
30. Borroff, *Language and the Poet,* p. 106.
31. *A Marianne Moore Reader* (New York: Viking, 1961), pp. 221–222.
32. Robert Pinsky, *The Situation of Poetry* (Princeton: Princeton University Press, 1976), p. 7.
33. Costello, *Marianne Moore: Imaginary Possessions*, pp. 52–53.
34. William Carlos Williams, "Marianne Moore," reprinted in Tomlinson, *Marianne Moore: A Collection*, p. 87.
35. Ibid, p. 58.
36. Pinsky, *The Situation of Poetry,* p. 4.

Chapter 2

1. George Herbert, "Affliction (I)," *The Works of George Herbert*, ed. F. E. Hutchinson (Oxford: Clarendon Press, 1941).

All subsequent quotations from Herbert's poems are from this text.

2. Dante, *La Vita Nuova*, trans. Barbara Reynolds (New York: Penguin Books, 1969), p. 29.

3. Elizabeth Bishop, Notebook 1. Rare Books and Manuscripts, Vassar College Library, Poughkeepsie, N.Y.

4. Bishop to Moore, 14 May 1942. (Rosenbach V:05:03.)

5. Bishop to Robert Lowell, Sunday 11th, 1957 (no month given). Houghton Library, Harvard University, Cambridge, Mass.

6. Elizabeth Bishop, "Influences," *The American Poetry Review* (January/February, 1985): p. 11.

7. Robert Giroux, Introduction to *Elizabeth Bishop: The Collected Prose* (New York: Farrar, Straus & Giroux, 1984), p. ix.

8. David Kalstone, "Elizabeth Bishop: Questions of Memory, Questions of Travel," *Five Temperaments* (New York: Oxford University Press, 1977), p. 13. (Reprinted in *Elizabeth Bishop and Her Art,* eds. Lloyd Schwartz and Sybil P. Estess, Ann Arbor, University of Michigan Press, 1983, pp. 3–31.)

9. Bishop, "Influences," p. 13.

10. Robert Dale Parker discusses the Bishop poem and alludes glancingly to the Herbert in "Bishop and the Weed of Poetic Invention," the first chapter of his book *The Unbeliever: The Poetry of Elizabeth Bishop* (Urbana: University of Illinois Press, 1988). In his recent book on Bishop, Thomas J. Travisano compares these two Bishop and Herbert poems. See Thomas J. Travisano, *Elizabeth Bishop: Her Artistic Development* (Charlottesville: University Press of Virginia, 1988), pp. 33–36. Both books were published after I had completed this chapter.

11. Ashley Brown, "An Interview with Elizabeth Bishop," in *Elizabeth Bishop and Her Art*, eds. Lloyd Schwartz and Sybil P. Estess (Ann Arbor: University of Michigan Press, 1983), p. 294.

12. See, for just a few examples, John Donne's "A Valediction: of Weeping," Richard Crashaw's "The Weeper," Andrew Marvell's "On a Drop of Dew," and Henry Vaughan's "The Showre."

13. Bishop, "Influences," p. 11.

14. Richard Howard, "Comment," *Preferences*, eds. Richard

Howard and Thomas Victor (New York: Viking, 1974), p. 31.

15. The single phrase that Bishop quotes from Herbert in a poem of her own is a poignant expression of that psychological strife in Herbert's poetry which she found compelling. Addressing his Lord in "Affliction (IV)," the troubled speaker says, "My thoughts are all a case of knives." Bishop transposes Herbert's metaphor in her "Wading at Wellfleet," where "all a case of knives" becomes a descriptive epithet for the sea's glittering waves.

16. William Nestrick, " 'Mine and Thine' in *The Temple*," in *"Too Rich To Clothe The Sunne": Essays on George Herbert*, eds. Claude J. Summers and Ted-Larry Pebworth (Pittsburgh: University of Pittsburgh Press, 1980), pp. 115–128.

17. René Wellek, "Romanticism Re-Examined," in *Romanticism Reconsidered*, ed. Northrop Frye (New York: Columbia University Press, 1963), p. 132.

18. Robert Pinsky, "The Idiom of a Self: Elizabeth Bishop and Wordsworth," in *Elizabeth Bishop and Her Art,* eds. Lloyd Schwartz and Sibyl P. Estess (Ann Arbor: University of Michigan Press, 1983), p. 49.

19. Helen Gardner quotes Aldous Huxley on Herbert in her Introduction to *The Poems of George Herbert* (New York: Oxford University Press, 1961), p. xv.

20. Kalstone, "Elizabeth Bishop," p. 40.

21. Helen Vendler, "Domestication, Domesticity, and the Otherworldly," in *Part of Nature*, *Part of Us* (Cambridge: Harvard University Press, 1980), p. 97. (Reprinted in Schwartz and Estess, *Elizabeth Bishop and Her Art,* pp. 32–48.)

22. Robert Lowell credits Bishop with influencing his manner in "On 'Skunk Hour,' " (reprinted in Schwartz and Estess, *Elizabeth Bishop and Her Art,* p. 199): "The dedication is to Elizabeth Bishop, because rereading her suggested a way of breaking through the shell of my old manner. Her rhythms, idiom, images, and stanza structure seemed to belong to a later century. 'Skunk Hour' is modelled on Miss Bishop's 'The Armadillo,' a much better poem and one I had heard her read and had later carried around with me." The question of who influences whom in the Bishop/Lowell friendship is complex, since the two exchanged letters and poems

and saw one another with some frequency in the late 1950s. See also Ian Hamilton's *Robert Lowell, A Biography* (New York: Random House, 1982).

23. Brown, "An Interview," Schwartz and Estess, *Elizabeth Bishop and Her Art,* p. 294.

24. These words, representing opposing poetic and moral values, appear in "Jordan (II)": "Curling with metaphors a plain intention." The word "plain" everywhere in Herbert denotes a fitting moral and aesthetic stance, while "curled" is generally charged with negative connotations (see his poems "The Starre" and "Dulness").

25. Yvor Winters, *Forms of Discovery* (Chicago: Alan Swallow, 1967), p. 84. Winters is partial to Herbert's "Church Monuments," which he says "might be described as the last word in the sophistication of the plain style."

26. Bishop to Moore, 31 January 1938. (Rosenbach: V:05:01.)

27. T. S. Eliot, "Andrew Marvell," in *Selected Essays* (New York: Harcourt, Brace, & Co., 1932), p. 262.

28. Hugh Kenner, *Seventeenth Century Poetry: The Schools of Donne and Jonson* (New York: Holt, Rinehart & Winston, 1964), p. 199.

29. David Kalstone quotes a 1948 letter from Bishop to Lowell in "Prodigal Years: Elizabeth Bishop and Robert Lowell, 1947–1949," *Grand Street* 4, no. 4 (Summer 1985): p. 176: "The water looks like blue gas—the harbor is always a mess here, junky little boats all piled up, some hung with sponges and always a few half sunk or splintered up from the most recent hurricane—it reminds me a little of my desk."

30. Bishop journal entry from July 1934 (Rare Books and Manuscripts, Vassar College Library, Poughkeepsie, N.Y.). Bishop's remark about "the dangers of love poetry" invites comparison of this young poet with the young George Herbert, who renounced secular love poetry. Bishop, of course, wrote poignant love poems such as "Insomnia" and "One Art"—and these are characterized by extreme formal control and emotional reticence. Alan Williamson has written on Bishop's uneasy relation to this genre in "*A Cold Spring:* The Poet of Feeling," Schwartz and Estess, *Elizabeth Bishop and Her Art,* pp. 96–108.

31. In her notes on Loyola dated 23 November 1934 (Rare

Books and Manuscripts, Vassar College Library, Poughkeepsie, N.Y.), Bishop cites the following passages, interesting
both in regard to her own descriptive/meditative practices
and in regard to her propensity, over the years, for composing "morning poems" or aubades:

> "The first prelude is a composition, seeing the place.—Here is to
> be observed that in contemplation, or visible meditation . . .
> the composition will be to see with the eye of the imagination
> the corporeal place where there is found the object which I wish
> to contemplate."
>
> Additions for improving exercises—
>
> 1. Before going to sleep, to think of the time of getting up "and
>   to what purpose."
> 2. On waking up "not giving place to these or those thoughts,
>   immediately to advert to what I am about to contemplate."

32. William Carlos Williams, "Marianne Moore," reprinted in
    Marianne Moore: A Collection of Critical Essays, ed. Charles
    Tomlinson (Englewood Cliffs, N.J.: Prentice-Hall, 1969), p.
    87.
33. Richard Strier, *Love Known: Theology and Experience in
    George Herbert's Poetry* (Chicago: University of Chicago
    Press, 1983), p. 191.
34. In *Self-Consuming Artifacts* (Berkeley: University of California
    Press, 1972), Stanley Fish considers the poem's central issue
    the question of agency. He sees Herbert's self-consciously
    ingenious pattern poem as gradually establishing what we
    might call its own pre-cision, its status as an artifact already
    carved on the human heart, already written by God:

> A broken ALTAR, Lord, thy servant reares,
> Made of a heart, and cemented with teares:
> Whose parts are as thy hand did frame;
> No workmans tools hath touch'd the same.
> > A HEART alone
> > Is such a stone,
> > As nothing but
> > Thy pow'r doth cut.

Assuming that "the altar in the poem and the altar that is
the poem" (the human heart and the work of art) are always
being referred to simultaneously, Fish argues that this first

half of Herbert's poem leads speaker and reader from an assertion of human ingenuity ("thy servant reares") and toward acknowledgment of the true authorship of God ("Thy pow'r doth cut"). Strier, on the other hand, sees in these same lines not an identity of heart/altar/poem, but rather a disjunction between the unbroken classical altar of the shaped poem and that other altar under discussion, the speaker's "broken and contrite heart." In Strier's view, "the central issue of the poem can more properly be seen as the relationship between the art it displays and the art it discusses—the relationship, in other words, not between its authors but between its altars." His reading of the concluding couplet, accordingly, differs radically from Fish's:

> O let thy blessed *sacrifice* be mine
> And sanctifie this *altar* to be thine.

"This Altar," Strier asserts, refers here not to the speaker's poem but only to his heart; and the point of the concluding couplet is not, as Fish suggests, a final self-reflexive abrogation of authorship, but rather a self-reflective *cri de coeur.* Strier's reading, then, primarily differs from Fish's in that it focusses more on emotion than on invention, more on the state of the heart than the status of art.

Both these critics nevertheless agree that Herbert's shaped poem is not a paean to human ingenuity; rather, it posits the limits of human art and the limitlessness of God's power.

35. Sybil P. Estess, "Description and Imagination in Elizabeth Bishop's 'The Map,' " Schwartz and Estess, *Elizabeth Bishop and Her Art,* p. 222.

36. Kalstone, "Elizabeth Bishop," p. 28.

37. According to *The Oxford Dictionary of English Etymology*, ed. E. T. Onions (Oxford University Press, 1966), the word *dubious* comes from the Latin for *two* and means "hesitating between two alternatives." Bishop revises her own phrasing in this poem in a manner that shows characteristic indecisiveness or hesitation: "Everything was withdrawn as far as possible,/indrawn"; "a track of big dog-prints (so big/they were more like lion-prints)"; "I'd like to retire there and do *nothing,*/or nothing much."

38. In "The Double Pleasures of Herbert's 'Collar' " (Summers

and Pebworth, "*Too Rich To Clothe The Sunne*," pp. 77–88), Ilona Bell remarks that "where Donne's mode is generally imperative, Herbert's is essentially interrogative." For a discussion of the importance of questions in Bishop's poetry, see Bonnie Costello's essay "The Impersonal and the Interrogative in the Poetry of Elizabeth Bishop," Schwartz and Estess, *Elizabeth Bishop and Her Art,* pp. 109–132.

Chapter 3

1. The four versions of this poem I discuss are (in chronological order):

   "A Graveyard in the Middle of the Sea" (draft, Rosenbach Museum and Library, Philadelphia).
   "A Graveyard," *Profile: An Anthology Collected in MCMXXXI,* by Ezra Pound (Milan: John Schweiwiller, 1932), pp. 59–60.
   "A Graveyard," *The Dial* LXXI, no. 1 (July 1921): p. 34.
   "A Grave," *Observations* (New York: Dial Press, 1924), reprinted in *The Complete Poems of Marianne Moore* (New York: Macmillan/Viking, 1981), p. 49.

2. Adrienne Rich is the originator of the charged term. See "When We Dead Awaken: Writing as Re-Vision (1971)," in *On Lies, Secrets, and Silence* (New York: Norton, 1979).

3. See Bonnie Costello, "The 'Feminine' Language of Marianne Moore," in *Women and Language in Literature and Society,* eds. Sally McConnell-Ginet, Ruth Borker, and Nelly Furman (New York: Praeger, 1980), pp. 222–238, and Alicia Ostriker, "What Do Women (Poets) Want?: Marianne Moore and H.D. as Poetic Ancestresses," *Poesis* 6, no. 3 & 4 (double issue) (1985): pp. 1–9. Moore appears as a stronger feminist presence in this essay than in Ostriker's later book, *Stealing the Language,* which I discuss in Chapter 5. Since I completed this chapter, some feminist critics have begun to locate in Moore a subtle feminist subversiveness (see note 4 to my Introduction).

4. T. S. Eliot, review of *Poems* and *Marriage, The Dial* LXXV (December 1923). (Reprinted in *Marianne Moore: A Collection of Critical Essays,* ed. Charles Tomlinson, Englewood Cliffs, N.J.: Prentice Hall, 1969, p. 51.)

5. Gorham B. Munson, *Destinations: A Canvass of American*

Literature Since 1900 (New York: AMS Press, 1970), p. 92. (Reprinted from the 1928 edition published by J. H. Sears & Co.)

6. John Unterecker, Foreword to *Marianne Moore: An Introduction to the Poetry*, by George W. Nitchie (New York: Columbia University Press, 1969).

7. Roy Harvey Pearce, *The Continuity of American Poetry* (Princeton: Princeton University Press, 1961), pp. 366–75.

8. Suzanne Juhasz, *Naked and Fiery Forms: Modern American Poetry by Women* (New York: Harper & Row, 1976), pp. 33–56.

9. Rich, *On Lies,* p. 39.

10. Ostriker, "What Do Women (Poets) Want?" p. 3. Ostriker is here describing the work of H.D. as well as that of Marianne Moore.

11. Hugh Kenner, "Disliking It," *A Homemade World* (New York: William Morrow, 1975), p. 98. Kenner reminds his reader that for a time Moore taught typewriting and then asserts that "the words on these pages [of Moore's poems] are little regular blocks, set apart by spaces, and referrable less to the voice than to the click of the keys and the ratcheting of the carriage."

12. Laurence Stapleton, *Marianne Moore: The Poet's Advance* (Princeton: Princeton University Press, 1978), p. 20.

13. *Edgar Allen Poe: Poetry and Tales*, selected by Patrick F. Quinn (New York: Literary Classics of the United States/Viking, 1984), p. 67.

14. Sandra M. Gilbert and Susan Gubar, *The Madwoman in the Attic* (New Haven: Yale University Press, 1979). See especially Chapter 2, "Infection in the Sentence: The Woman Writer and the Anxiety of Authorship."

15. *The Letters of Ezra Pound*, ed. D. D. Paige (New York: New Directions, 1950), pp. 141–143.

16. Moore to Pound, 9 January 1919, in Tomlinson, *Marianne Moore: A Collection,* pp. 16–19.

17. Margaret Homans, *Women Writers and Poetic Identity* (Princeton: Princeton University Press, 1980), p. 12.

18. E. de Selincourt and Helen Darbishire, eds., *The Poetical Works of William Wordsworth,* 5 vols. (Oxford: Clarendon Press, 1940–1949; p. 149). (Reprinted 1966.)

19. In "Virginia Britannia," composed nearly twenty years after "A Grave," Moore directly alludes to Wordsworth's immortality ode: her last line describes clouds at sunset above Virginia, and claims they "are to the child an intimation of what glory is" (CPMM, p. 107). The form of the poem also loosely imitates Wordsworth's ode form. Writing at length on this poem and others from Moore's "Old Dominion" sequence, which first appeared in *The Pangolin and Other Verse* (1936), John M. Slatin discusses these poems' "complex and ironic relationship to the tradition of the Romantic Ode," arguing for the greater complexity and originality of the earlier version of "Virginia Britannia" (*The Savage's Romance*, University Park: Pennsylvania State University, 1986, p. 211). In both versions, Moore's adaptations of Wordsworth seem to me a way of linking his poetics to the equivocal "glory" of Virginia's history—that is, to the rapaciousness of British colonialism and the "arrogance" of the modern state, as well as to the accomplishment of the culturally mixed, "indivisible" new nation that the colony adumbrated. Yet both versions conclude by using Wordsworthian phrasing to insist upon some higher "glory" distinct from *gloria mundi*. "A Grave" seems to me finally a fiercer, less conservative attempt on the younger poet's part to position herself in regard to Romantic nature poetry.

20. One might notice a similar idealization of the silenced or dead woman in Renaissance Petrarchan poetics. The Romantic poets, however, persistently conflate woman with idealized and imaginatively dominated nature.

21. Bonnie Costello, *Marianne Moore: Imaginary Possessions* (Cambridge, Mass.: Harvard University Press, 1981), p. 62.

22. One might note in this fatal *femme* context Moore's use of a quoted phrase in "Marriage" that her notes for the poem attribute to Ezra Pound: "a wife is a coffin." An interestingly related, contemporary expression of that morbid association is Louise Glück's assertion in "Dedication to Hunger" that "a woman's body/is a grave" (*Descending Figure*, New York: Ecco Press, 1980, p. 32).

23. Hugh Kenner gives a full and forceful exposition of "otherness" in Moore's poetry in "Disliking It," a chapter in his book *A Homemade World*, pp. 91–118.

24. Moore seems to have elicited in Pound anxiety about gender definitions as well as a defiant reassertion of bellicose masculine volition. His letter to her of 1 February 1919 begins with a long free-verse riff (*The Letters of Ezra Pound, 1907–1941*, ed. D. D. Paige, New York: Harcourt, Brace & Co., p. 146):

> The female is a chaos
>
>> the male
>
>> is a fixed point of stupidity, but only the female
> can content itself with prolonged conversation
> with but one sole other creature of its own sex
> and of its own unavoidable species
>
>> the male
>
>> is more expansive
> and demands other and varied contacts;
> hence its combativeness . . .

See also Pound's "Canto XXIX" (Ezra Pound, *Cantos,* New York: New Directions, 1970, p. 144):

> . . . the female
> Is an elephant, the female
> Is a chaos
> An octopus
> A biological process
>> and we seek to fulfill
> TAN AOIDAN, our desire, drift . . .

In "Image, Word, and Sign," *Critical Inquiry* 12, no. 2 (Winter 1986), p. 358, Michael André Bernstein observes Pound's obsession in the *Cantos* with "the engulfing dangers of an ungovernable female sexuality" and with "phallic male order."

25. Costello, *Marianne Moore: Imaginary Possessions*, p. 64.
26. I sense in the movement of these poems a certain anxiety about submerged sexuality. "A Grave" avoids a clear (and traditional) association of the sea's flux and flow with forces in the female *body*.
27. Costello, "The 'Feminine' Language," p. 64.
28. Costello cites this entry in *Marianne Moore: Imaginary Possessions* (p. 63), as Rosenbach 1250/2, 56, from *The Greek Anthology* II: p. 631. See *The Greek Anthology*, English trans. by W. R. Paton, 5 vols. (New York: G. P. Putnam, 1918).

29. Elizabeth Bishop, "Influences," reprinted in *The American Poetry Review* (January/February, 1985), pp. 11–16.

Chapter 4

1. Elizabeth Bishop, "Efforts of Affection," *Elizabeth Bishop: The Collected Prose*, ed. Robert Giroux (New York: Farrar, Straus & Giroux, 1984), p. 133. Subsequent references to this book appear in text abbreviated CPrEB.
2. Letter to Robert Lowell, 11 July 1951. Houghton Library, Harvard University, Cambridge, Mass.
3. Bishop had won the Houghton Mifflin poetry award in 1946 for her first book, *North & South*, but in that same year Lowell had made his more glorious mark with the Pulitzer-Prize-winning *Lord Weary's Castle*. At the time of this letter, Lowell, six years her junior, was traveling in Europe after completing his third volume, while she was still struggling at home with her second.
4. Rare Books and Manuscripts, Vassar College Library, Poughkeepsie, N.Y.
5. Wordsworth's notes on his poems, dictated to Isabella Fenwick in 1843, repeatedly credit Dorothy as a source. "Lucy Gray," for example, was "founded on a circumstance told me by my sister" (*Poetical Works* of 1857).
6. Robert Pinsky, "The Idiom of a Self," *Elizabeth Bishop and Her Art*, eds. Lloyd Schwartz and Sybil P. Estess (Ann Arbor: The University of Michigan Press, 1983), p. 56.
7. Willard Spiegelman, "Elizabeth Bishop's 'Natural Heroism'," Schwartz and Estess, *Elizabeth Bishop and Her Art,* p. 154.
8. George Starbuck, " 'The Work!': A Conversation with Elizabeth Bishop," *Ploughshares* 3, nos. 3 & 4 (1977). (Reprinted in Schwartz and Estess, *Elizabeth Bishop and Her Art,* p. 329.)
9. Sandra M. Gilbert and Susan Gubar, *The Madwoman in the Attic* (New Haven: Yale University Press, 1979), p. 49.
10. Harold Bloom, *The Visionary Company: A Reading of English Romantic Poetry* (Ithaca: Cornell University Press, rev. ed. 1971), pp. 131–164.

11. Ashley Brown, "An Interview with Elizabeth Bishop," Schwartz and Estess, *Elizabeth Bishop and Her Art,* p. 295.
12. E. de Selincourt and Helen Darbishire, eds., *The Poetical Works of William Wordsworth,* 5 vols. (Oxford: Clarendon Press, 1940–1949; reprinted 1966). Subsequent quotations of Wordsworth's poetry are from the 1966 edition.
13. Ashley Brown, "An Interview," p. 296.
14. See Carol T. Christ, *Victorian and Modern Poetics* (Chicago: University of Chicago Press, 1984), pp. 2–3: "The Victorians and the Modernists find the prominence which they feel that Romanticism gives to the poet's subjectivity burdensome and restrictive. Even while they write within a Romantic tradition, each of the major Victorian and Modernist poets reacts against the subjectivity which he associates with Romanticism by attempting to objectify the materials of poetry."
15. Penelope Laurans, " 'Old Correspondences': Prosodic Transformations in Elizabeth Bishop," Schwartz and Estess, *Elizabeth Bishop and Her Art,* p. 90.
16. Laurans, " 'Old Correspondences,' " p. 76.
17. A.R.C. Finch, "Dickinson and Patriarchal Meter: A Theory of Metrical Codes," *PMLA* 102, no. 2 (March 1987): p. 168.
18. Pinsky, "The Idiom of a Self," Schwartz and Estess, *Elizabeth Bishop and Her Art,* p. 56.
19. Letter to Marianne Moore, 24 October 1954. (Rosenbach: V:05:04.)
20. Ezra Pound, "Canto LXXXI," *Cantos* (New York: New Directions, 1970).
21. Gilbert and Gubar, *Madwoman,* p. 73.
22. Letter to Marianne Moore, 5 December 1936.
23. Robert Pinsky, "Geographer of the Self," *The New Republic* (April 4, 1983): p. 25.
24. Bloom, *The Visionary Company,* p. 125.
25. Ibid, p. 144.
26. Elizabeth Spires, "The Art of Poetry XXVII," an interview with Elizabeth Bishop in *The Paris Review* 22, no. 80 (Summer 1981): p. 80. Defending Moore's poetry against early feminist critics, Bishop asks in her memoir "Efforts of Affection": "Do they know that Marianne Moore was a feminist

in her day? Or that she paraded with the suffragettes led by Inez Milholland on her white horse, down Fifth Avenue? Once, Marianne told me, she 'climbed a lamppost' in a demonstration for votes for women." (CPrEB, p. 144)

27. The seeming obliviousness of Wordsworth's speaker to the leech-gatherer's separate experience is parodied by Lewis Carroll in his verse "The White Knight's Song."

28. Spiegelman, "Elizabeth Bishop's 'Natural Heroism,' " Schwartz and Estess, *Elizabeth Bishop and Her Art*, p. 167.

29. For a discussion of Bishop's evasion of gender determination in response to the American sublime, see Joanne Feit Diehl, "At Home with Loss: Elizabeth Bishop and the American Sublime," *Coming to Light: American Women Poets in the Twentieth Century*, eds. Diane Wood Middlebrook and Marilyn Yalom (Ann Arbor: University of Michigan Press, 1985), pp. 123–137.

30. Bishop described Aruba in letters to Robert Lowell of 14 December 1957 and 26 April 1962, remarking in the latter that "nothing could be worse than Aruba," and mentioning goats and "volcanoes, tiny ones" (Houghton Library, Harvard University, Cambridge, Mass.). In her interview with George Starbuck in 1977, she makes this connection between *her* Crusoe's island and Aruba explicit:

> GS: What got the Crusoe poem started?
> EB: I don't know. I reread the book and discovered how really awful Robinson Crusoe was, which I hadn't realized. I hadn't read it in a long time. And then I was remembering a visit to Aruba—long before it was developed as a "resort." I took a trip across the island and it's true that there are small volcanoes all over the place. [Schwartz and Estess, *Elizabeth Bishop and Her Art*, p. 319]

31. We might also see Bishop's short, often roughly three-beat lines as her adaptation of George Herbert's meters. If we view adapted hymn or ballad meter in her work as an alternative to iambic pentameter, so closely connected with the male-dominated poetic tradition, Wordsworth would then seem to offer a conflicted metrical model, and Herbert, with his characteristic mixed meters, perhaps a more consistently "nonpatriarchal" alternative. See A.R.C. Finch's article "Dickinson and Patriarchal Meter" for a discussion of

Emily Dickinson's use of hymn meter as an alternative to patriarchal pentameter and her use of iambic pentameter as a "signifying code."

Chapter 5

1. Elizabeth Bishop describes Mrs. Moore in "Efforts of Affection" (CPrEB, p. 129):

   > Mrs. Moore was in her seventies when I first knew her, very serious—solemn, rather—although capable of irony, and very devout. . . . Her manner toward Marianne was that of a kindly, self-controlled parent who felt that she had to take a firm line, that her daughter might be given to flightiness or—an equal sin, in her eyes—mistakes in grammar. She had taught English at a girls' school and her sentences were Johnsonian in weight and balance. . . . Waiting for the conclusion of her longer statements, I grew rather nervous; nevertheless, I found her extreme precision enviable and thought I could detect echoes of Marianne's own style in it: the use of double or triple negatives, the lighter and wittier ironies—Mrs. Moore had provided a sort of ground bass for them."

2. Ezra Pound, "The Renaissance," *Literary Essays*, ed. T. S. Eliot (New York: New Directions, 1968), p. 214. ("The Renaissance" was first published in *Poetry* in 1914.)

3. *Marianne Moore Newsletter*, 5, no. 1 (Spring 1981): p. 17.

4. "Interview with Donald Hall," *A Marianne Moore Reader* (New York: Viking, 1961), p. 257.

5. Moore's copy of Browne's miscellaneous writings is at the Rosenbach Museum and Library, Philadelphia. (Moore Library RC2 5/34.)

6. Bonnie Costello, "Marianne Moore's Wild Decorum," *The American Poetry Review* 16, no. 2 (March/April 1987): p. 47.

7. In juxtaposing "digressive" and "directive," I have borrowed Costello's apt phrasing ("Marianne Moore's Wild Decorum," p. 49).

8. Letter from Bishop to Moore, 24 October 1954. (Rosenbach V:05:04.)

9. Letter from Moore to Bishop, 20 September 1936.

10. Robert Frost, *The Poetry of Robert Frost*, ed. Edward Connery Lathem (New York: Holt, Rinehart & Winston, 1969),

pp. 251–252. Frost's poem, from *West-Running Brook* (1928), was first published in *The Yale Review* in July 1927—the same year, presumably, that the youthful Bishop drafted her poem.

11. Elizabeth Bishop, "As We Like It," *Quarterly Review of Literature* 4 (Spring 1948): pp. 129–135.

12. For an interesting discussion of Moore's impact on Bishop's descriptive development, as evinced in the Moore and Bishop correspondence, see Lynn Keller's "Words Worth a Thousand Postcards: The Bishop/Moore Correspondence," *American Literature* 55, no. 3 (October 1983): pp. 405–429.

13. Moore singles out this poem for praise in letters of 11 July 1936, 21 March 1942, and 5 November 1944. In the 1936 letter she attributes to " 'The Imaginary Iceberg,' and others I have seen—a certain satisfactory doughtiness."

14. Moore to Bishop, 7 March 1937.

15. Moore to Bishop, 1 May 1938.

16. Bishop's later poetry is more autobiographical than her early work, a change in poetic practice that may—as David Kalstone remarked to me in a conversation of 16 December 1984—show the influence of Lowell's *Life Studies*. But Bishop's autobiographical or semiautobiographical poems remain mysterious, and assiduously avoid many intimate details. Bishop expressed a distaste for the confessional mode, both in her private correspondence with Lowell and in public statements: "You just wish," she remarked, "they'd keep some of these things to themselves." See "Poets," *Time*, June 2, 1967, reprinted in *Elizabeth Bishop and Her Art*, eds. Lloyd Schwartz and Sybil P. Estess (Ann Arbor: University of Michigan Press, 1983), p. 303.

17. George Starbuck, " 'The Work!': A Conversation with Elizabeth Bishop," *Ploughshares* 3, nos. 3 & 4 (1977). (Reprinted in Schwartz and Estess, *Elizabeth Bishop and Her Art*, p. 327.)

18. John Ashbery, "The Complete Poems," Schwartz and Estess, *Elizabeth Bishop and Her Art*, pp. 201–202.

19. Harold Bloom, *The Anxiety of Influence* (New York: Oxford University Press, 1973), p. 25.

20. Ibid., p. 11.

21. Ibid., p. 5.

22. Wallace Stevens, *The Collected Poems* (New York: Knopf, 1975), pp. 69–70.
23. Bloom, *American Women Poets* (New York: Chelsea House, 1986), p. 2.
24. Ibid., p. 8. The quotation comes from the Emily Dickinson poem beginning "The Tint I cannot take — is best."
25. Emily Dickinson, who might seem the obvious choice, appears to have been a *primary* influence for neither Moore nor Bishop—perhaps because in their youth her poetry was available only in reworked early editions that tended to emphasize the sentimental and the fey. In her interview with George Starbuck, Bishop remarked: "I had (at the age of twelve) read Emily Dickinson, but an early edition, and I didn't like it much" (Schwartz and Estess, *Elizabeth Bishop and Her Art,* p. 319). In her memoir "Efforts of Affection" Bishop remarks, "I do not remember her [Marianne Moore] ever referring to Emily Dickinson" (CPrEB, p. 143). For a reading that assumes Dickinson as an important source for Bishop, see Harold Bloom's introduction to *American Women Poets.*
26. Schwartz and Estess, *Elizabeth Bishop and Her Art,* p. 322.
27. To their credit, Sandra M. Gilbert and Susan Gubar cite this letter in *The Norton Anthology of Literature by Women* (New York: Norton, 1985), p. 1739.
28. Margaret Homans, *Women Writers and Poetic Identity* (Princeton: Princeton University Press, 1980), p. 8.
29. Sandra M. Gilbert and Susan Gubar, *No Man's Land: The Place of the Woman Writer in the Twentieth Century,* vol. 1, *The War of the Words* (New Haven: Yale University Press, 1988).
30. Sandra M. Gilbert and Susan Gubar, *The Madwoman in the Attic* (New Haven: Yale University Press, 1979), p. 80.
31. Ibid., p. 73.
32. Ibid., p. xi.
33. Ibid., p. 59.
34. Ellen Moers, *Literary Women* (New York: Doubleday, 1976).
35. Gilbert and Gubar's *Madwoman* has been the subject of a number of critiques from a variety of perspectives. See, for some examples:

Rosemary Dinnage, "Re-creating Eve," *The New York Review of Books* 26 (December 1979): pp. 6–8.

Mary Jacobus, review of *The Madwoman in the Attic* and *Shakespeare's Sisters*, *Signs* 6, no. 3 (Spring 1981): pp. 517–523.

Frank Lentricchia in "Patriarchy Against Itself—The Young Manhood of Wallace Stevens," *Critical Inquiry* 13 (Summer 1987): pp. 742–786. And see also Gilbert and Gubar's response, entitled "The Man on the Dump versus the United Dames of America; or, What Does Frank Lentricchia Want?" in *Critical Inquiry* 14 (Winter 1988): pp. 386–413.

Toril Moi, "Women Writing and Writing About Women," *Sexual/Textual Politics: Feminist Literary Theory* (New York: Methuen, 1985), pp. 50–69.

36. Gilbert and Gubar, *Madwoman*, p. xiii.

37. Ibid., pp. 71–72.

38. Jan Montefiore, *Feminism and Poetry* (New York: Pandora, 1987), p. 5.

39. Adrienne Rich, *On Lies, Secrets, and Silence: Selected Prose 1966–1978* (New York: Norton, 1979), p. 35.

40. Ibid., p. 39.

41. Ibid., p. 44.

42. Ibid., p. 49.

43. Ibid., p. 43.

44. Ibid., p. 43.

45. Adrienne Rich, "The Eye of the Outsider: Elizabeth Bishop's *Complete Poems, 1927–1979*," *Blood, Bread, and Poetry: Selected Prose 1979–1985* (New York: Norton, 1986), p. 127.

46. Alicia Suskin Ostriker, *Stealing the Language: The Emergence of Women's Poetry in America* (Boston: Beacon Press, 1986).

47. Ibid., p. 211.

48. Marjorie Perloff, "Recharging the Canon: Some Reflections on Feminist Poetics and the Avant-Garde," *American Poetry Review* (July-August 1986): p. 13.

49. Ostriker, *Stealing the Language*, p. 54.

50. Ibid., p. 55.

51. Ibid., p. 209.

52. Susan Schweik, "An Oblique Place: Elizabeth Bishop and the Language of War," *A Gulf So Deeply Cut: American Women Poets and the Second World War* (forthcoming).

53. See Lorrie Goldensohn, "Elizabeth Bishop: An Unpublished, Untitled Poem," *American Poetry Review* (January/February 1988): pp. 35–46.

54. Schweik, in "An Oblique Place," suggests that Bishop's "Roosters" may be read, among other things, as a "lesbian aubade."

55. Ostriker, *Stealing the Language,* p. 118.

56. Ibid., p. 119.

57. See Helen Vendler, *Part of Nature, Part of Us* (Cambridge, Mass.: Harvard University Press, 1980), pp. 109–110.

58. Ostriker, *Stealing the Language,* p. 119.

59. Ibid., p. 193.

60. Ibid., p. 16. Betsy Erkkila proposes the Demeter/Kore model of female literary influence in "Dickinson and Rich: Toward a Theory of Female Poetic Influence," *American Literature* 56, no. 4 (December 1984): pp. 541–559.

61. Ibid., p. ix: "First among poets in my life is William Blake, rule-breaker and revolutionary. . . . To study Blake is to acquire an appetite for the conceptually and emotionally difficult in poetry, and a thirst for the visionary."

62. Gilbert and Gubar, *No Man's Land,* p. 168.

63. Ibid., pp. 212–214.

64. Ibid., p. xiv.

65. Ibid., p. 169.

66. Moore to Hildegarde Watson, 30 November 1941. Eileen G. Moran, "Selected Letters of Marianne Moore to Hildegarde Watson, ed., with an Introduction," dissertation, Bryn Mawr, 1984, p. 193.

67. For a discussion of the dynamics of women's friendships as they shape and are shaped by the contemporary female literary imagination, see Elizabeth Abel's "(E)Merging Identities: The Dynamics of Female Friendship in Contemporary Fiction by Women," *Signs* (Spring 1981):413–435.

68. Joanne Feit Diehl discusses Dickinson's anxious, ambivalent relation to a powerful male "Composite Precursor," or muse, who is associated with father, lover, and God. " 'Come Slowly—Eden': An Exploration of Women Poets and Their Muse," *Signs* (Spring 1978): pp. 572–587.

69. Costello, "Marianne Moore's Wild Decorum," p. 50.

70. See, for example, Suzanne Juhasz, *Naked and Fiery Forms,*

Modern American Poetry by Women (New York: Harper & Row, 1976).

71. Marianne Moore, "Black Earth," *Poems* (London: Egoist Press, 1921).

72. A case may be made that Swinburne's use of "man" means specifically and only that, and that Moore's silent assent to his usage is an example of collusion with oppressive patriarchy. But this was, after all, the early twenties after a flush of effective feminism, and educated women did not then choose the limited use of "man" as an important topic for argument. They still believed that the word could be construed generically, for both sexes. (For the generic usage in Moore's poetry, see "The Pangolin": "Bedizened or stark/naked, man, the self, the being we call human, writing-/master to this world. . . ." For a double-edged usage see "A Grave": "Man looking into the sea . . .")

73. Elizabeth Bishop, *The Diary of "Helena Morley"* (New York: Ecco Press, 1977), p. 143.

Selected Bibliography

Marianne Moore: Primary Sources

Poems. London: Egoist Press, 1921.
Marriage. New York: Manikin Number Three, Monroe Wheeler, 1923.
Observations. New York: The Dial Press, 1924.
Reviews and Comments in *The Dial*, 1921–1929.
Selected Poems. New York: Macmillan, 1935.
The Pangolin and Other Verse. London: Brendin, 1936.
What Are Years? New York: Macmillan, 1941.
Nevertheless. New York: Macmillan, 1944.
Collected Poems. New York: Macmillan, 1951.
The Fables of La Fontaine. London: Faber & Faber, 1954.
Predilections. New York: Viking, 1955.
Like a Bulwark. New York: Viking, 1956.
O to Be a Dragon. New York: Viking, 1959.
A Marianne Moore Reader. New York: Viking, 1961.
The Arctic Ox. London: Faber & Faber, 1964.
Tell Me, Tell Me: Granite, Steele, and Other Topics. New York: Viking, 1966.
The Complete Poems of Marianne Moore. New York: Macmillan/Viking, 1967.

Unfinished Poems by Marianne Moore. Philadelphia: Rosenbach Museum and Library, 1972.

The Complete Poems of Marianne Moore. New York: Macmillan/ Viking, 1981.

The Complete Prose of Marianne Moore. Edited by Patricia C. Willis. New York: Viking, 1986.

Notebooks and letters from the Marianne Moore Collection at The Rosenbach Museum and Library, Philadelphia. Marianne C. Moore, literary executor.

Moore's letters to Elizabeth Bishop from the Department of Rare Books and Manuscripts, Vassar College Library, Poughkeepsie, N.Y. Alice Methfessel, literary executor.

Marianne Moore: Secondary Sources

Abbott, Craig S. *Marianne Moore: A Descriptive Bibliography*. Pittsburgh: University of Pittsburgh Press, 1977.

———. *Marianne Moore: A Reference Guide*. Boston: G. K. Hall, 1978.

Bishop, Elizabeth. "Efforts of Affection: A Memoir of Marianne Moore." In *Elizabeth Bishop: The Collected Prose,* edited by Robert Giroux, pp. 121–158. New York: Farrar, Straus & Giroux, 1984.

Bloom, Harold, ed. *Modern Critical Views: Marianne Moore*. New York: Chelsea House, 1987.

Bogan, Louise. *Achievement in American Poetry, 1900–1957*. Chicago: Henry Regnery, 1951.

Borroff, Marie. *Language and the Poet: Verbal Artistry in Frost, Stevens, and Moore*. Chicago: University of Chicago Press, 1979.

Costello, Bonnie. *Marianne Moore: Imaginary Possessions*. Cambridge, Mass.: Harvard University Press, 1981.

———. "Marianne Moore's Wild Decorum." *The American Poetry Review* 16, no. 2 (March/April 1987): pp. 43–54.

———. "The 'Feminine' Language of Marianne Moore." In *Women and Language in Literature and Society*, edited by Sally McConnell-Ginet, Ruth Borker, and Nelly Furman. New York: Praeger, 1980.

Engel, Bernard F. *Marianne Moore*. New York: Twayne, 1964.

Garrigue, Jean. *Marianne Moore*. University of Minnesota Pamphlets on American Writers, no. 50. Minneapolis: University of Minnesota Press, 1965.

Goodridge, Celeste, ed. *Sagetrieb* 6, no. 3 (Winter 1987). An issue devoted to a collection of essays on Moore.

Hadas, Pamela White. *Marianne Moore: Poet of Affection*. Syracuse, N.Y.: Syracuse University Press, 1977.

Hall, Donald. *Marianne Moore: The Cage and the Animal*. New York: Western Publishing, 1970.

Jackson, Thomas H., ed. *Poesis* 6, no. 3 & 4 (double issue) (1985). An issue devoted to a collection of essays on H.D. and Moore.

Jarrell, Randall. *Poetry and the Age*, pp. 162–188. New York: Vintage, 1953.

Kappell, Andrew J., ed. *Twentieth Century Literature: Marianne Moore Issue* 30, no. 2 and 3 (Summer/Fall 1984).

Kenner, Hugh. *A Homemade World: The American Modernist Writers*. New York: William Morrow, Inc., 1975.

Martin, Taffy. *Marianne Moore: Subversive Modernist*. Austin: University of Texas Press, 1986.

Nitchie, George W. *Marianne Moore: An Introduction to the Poetry*. New York: Columbia University Press, 1969.

Phillips, Elizabeth. *Marianne Moore*. New York: Frederick Ungar, 1982.

Schulman, Grace. *Marianne Moore: The Poetry of Engagement*. Urbana: University of Illinois Press, 1986.

Schweik, Susan. "Writing War Poetry Like a Woman," *Critical Inquiry* 13, no. 3 (Spring 1987): pp. 532–556.

Sheehy, Eugene P., and K. A. Lohf, comps. *The Achievement of Marianne Moore: A Bibliography 1907–1957*. New York: New York Public Library, 1958.

Slatin, John M. *The Savage's Romance: The Poetry of Marianne Moore*. University Park: Pennsylvania University Press, 1986.

Stapleton, Laurence. *Marianne Moore: The Poet's Advance*. Princeton: Princeton University Press, 1978.

Tambimuttu, ed. *Festschrift for Marianne Moore's Seventy-Seventh Birthday by Various Hands*. New York: Tambimuttu and Mass, 1964.

Therese, Sister M. *Marianne Moore: A Critical Essay*. Grand Rapids, Michigan: William Eerdmans, 1969.

Tomlinson, Charles, ed. *Marianne Moore: A Collection of Critical Essays.* Englewood Cliffs, N.J.: Prentice-Hall, 1969.

Vendler, Helen. *Part of Nature, Part of Us: Modern American Poets,* pp. 59–76. Cambridge, Mass.: Harvard University Press, 1980.

Weatherhead, A. Kingsley. *The Edge of the Image: Marianne Moore, William Carlos Williams, and Some Other Poets.* Seattle: University of Washington Press, 1967.

Willis, Patricia, ed. *Marianne Moore Newsletter.* Spring 1977 through Fall 1983. Philadelphia: Rosenbach Museum and Library.

Elizabeth Bishop: Primary Sources

North & South. Boston: Houghton Mifflin, 1946.

Poems: North & South—A Cold Spring. Boston: Houghton Mifflin, 1955.

Poems. London: Chatto & Windus, 1956. Selection of twenty poems from previous volumes.

The Diary of "Helena Morley." By Alice (Dayrell) Brant. Translated by Elizabeth Bishop. New York: Farrar, Straus & Cudahy, 1957. Reprint. New York: Ecco Press, 1977.

Brazil. By Elizabeth Bishop with the editors of *Life.* New York: Time-Life Books, 1962.

Questions of Travel. New York: Farrar, Straus & Giroux, 1965.

Selected Poems. London: Chatto & Windus, 1967.

The Ballad of the Burglar of Babylon. New York: Farrar, Straus & Giroux, 1968.

The Complete Poems. New York: Farrar, Straus & Giroux, 1969. Includes all the poems from *North & South, A Cold Spring,* and *Questions of Travel,* except for "The Mountain."

Anthology of Twentieth Century Brazilian Poetry. Edited by Elizabeth Bishop and Emanuel Brasil. Middletown, Conn.: Wesleyan University Press, 1972. Contains translations by Bishop.

Geography III. New York: Farrar, Straus & Giroux, 1976.

The Complete Poems 1927–1979. New York: Farrar, Straus & Giroux, 1983. Includes four new poems, previously uncollected and occasional poems, and thirteen poems written in youth.

Elizabeth Bishop: The Collected Prose. Edited by Robert Giroux. New York: Farrar, Straus & Giroux, 1984. Includes stories and memoirs, as well as Bishop's memoir of Marianne Moore.

"Influences," *American Poetry Review* 14 (January/February 1985): pp. 11–16. A posthumously printed, edited version of a talk Elizabeth Bishop gave on December 13, 1977, in a series entitled "Conversations" sponsored by the Academy of American Poets.

Unpublished drafts, some correspondence, and private journals in the Department of Rare Books and Manuscripts, Vassar College Library, Poughkeepsie, N.Y. Alice Methfessel, literary executor.

Bishop's letters to Marianne Moore in the Rosenbach Museum and Library, Philadelphia, Pa. Marianne C. Moore, literary executor.

Bishop's letters to Robert Lowell at the Houghton Library, Harvard University, Cambridge, Mass.

Elizabeth Bishop: Secondary Sources

Bromwich, David. "Elizabeth Bishop's Dream-Houses," *Raritan* 4, no. 1 (Summer 1984): pp. 77–91.

Diehl, Joanne Feit. "At Home with Loss: Elizabeth Bishop and the American Sublime." In *Coming to Light: American Women Poets in the Twentieth Century,* edited by Diane Wood Middlebrook and Marilyn Yalom, pp. 123–137. Ann Arbor: University of Michigan Press, 1985.

Kalstone, David. "Elizabeth Bishop: Questions of Memory, Questions of Travel." In *Five Temperaments,* pp. 12–40. New York: Oxford University Press, 1977.

———. "Prodigal Years: Elizabeth Bishop and Robert Lowell, 1947–1949," *Grand Street* 4, no. 4 (Summer 1985): pp. 170–193.

———. "Trial Balances: Elizabeth Bishop and Marianne Moore," *Grand Street* 3, no. 1 (Autumn 1983): pp. 115–135.

Keller, Lynn. "Words Worth a Thousand Postcards: The Bishop/Moore Correspondence," *American Literature* 55, no. 3 (October 1983): pp. 405–429.

————. *Re-Making It New*, Chapters 3 and 4. New York: Cambridge University Press, 1987.

Keller, Lynn and Cristanne Miller. "Emily Dickinson, Elizabeth Bishop, and the Rewards of Indirection," *The New England Quarterly* 57, no. 4 (December 1984): pp. 533–553.

Parker, Robert Dale. *The Unbeliever: The Poetry of Elizabeth Bishop*. Urbana: University of Illinois Press, 1988.

Perloff, Marjorie. "Elizabeth Bishop: The Course of a Particular," *Modern Poetry Studies* 8, no. 3 (1977): pp. 177–191.

Pinsky, Robert. "Poetry and the World." *Antaeus* 40 and 41 (Winter/Spring 1981). (Reprinted in Pinsky, R., *Poetry and the World*, New York, Ecco Press, 1988, pp. 3–17.)

————. "Geographer of the Self," *The New Republic* 4 (April 1983).

Schwartz, Lloyd, and Sybil P. Estess, eds. *Elizabeth Bishop and Her Art*. Ann Arbor: University of Michigan Press, 1983. Contains important critical essays, including essays by Helen Vendler, Robert Pinsky, Bonnie Costello, and David Kalstone; a chronology of reviews and tributes; a brief selection of remarks and occasional pieces by Bishop herself; two interviews with the poet; and a useful bibliography.

Spires, Elizabeth. "The Art of Poetry XXVII: Elizabeth Bishop," *The Paris Review* 22, no. 80 (Summer, 1981): pp. 57–83.

Stevenson, Anne. *Elizabeth Bishop*. New York: Twayne, 1966. Written prior to the 1965 publication of *Questions of Travel*.

Travisano, Thomas J. *Elizabeth Bishop: Her Artistic Development*. Charlottesville: University Press of Virginia, 1988.

Vendler, Helen. *Part of Nature, Part of Us*. Cambridge, Mass.: Harvard University Press, 1980.

Wylie, Diane E. *Elizabeth Bishop and Howard Nemerov: A Reference Guide*. Boston: G. K. Hall, 1983.

Index